100 Ideas for Secondary Teachers

Outstanding English Lessons

Other titles in the 100 Ideas for Secondary Teachers series:

100 Ideas for Secondary Teachers

Outstanding English Lessons

Angella Cooze and Mary Myatt

BLOOMSBURY

LONDON • NEW DELHI • NEW YORK • SYDNEY

Bloomsbury Education

An imprint of Bloomsbury Publishing Plc

50 Bedford Square
London
WC1B 3DP
UK

1385 Broadway
New York
NY 10018
USA

www.bloomsbury.com

Bloomsbury is a registered trade mark of Bloomsbury Publishing Plc

Published 2014

© Angella Cooze and Mary Myatt 2014

British Library Cataloguing-in-Publication Data
A catalogue record for this book is available from the British Library.

ISBN: PB: 9781408194935
ePub: 9781408194959
ePDF: 9781408194942

Library of Congress Cataloging-in-Publication Data
A catalog record for this book is available from the Library of Congress.

10 9 8 7 6 5 4 3 2

Typeset by Newgen Knowledge Works (P) Ltd., Chennai, India
Printed by CPI Group (UK) Ltd, Croydon, CR0 4YY

This book is produced using paper that is made from wood grown in managed, sustainable forests. It is natural, renewable and recyclable. The logging and manufacturing processes conform to the environmental regulations of the country of origin.

To view more of our titles please visit www.bloomsbury.com

Contents

Acknowledgements

Angella Cooze: This book owes a great deal to all of the excellent teachers (my husband included) I have worked with, trained students with and trained in my career so far. Their ideas and conversations (including, especially, the debates) have been invaluable to my own developing practice, as well as to those I have taught. Thank you.

Mary Myatt: There is great work being done in schools and I would like to thank all those who have welcomed me into their classrooms, let me talk to their students and look at their books.

And thanks too, to the virtual network of educators who are thinking hard, practising and blogging about what is working and more importantly what isn't. In particular @atharby @joe__kirby @LearningSpy @HuntingEnglish @headguruteacher @TeacherToolkit @imagineinquiry and @SurrealAnarchy for stimulating my thinking and letting me in on some great conversations.

And to John and Pauline Ward, inspirational teachers to thousands of students.

Introduction

This book has been written to help colleagues work smarter, not harder! We all need information and ideas and we often need them quickly. *100 Ideas for Secondary Teachers: Outstanding English Lessons* has strategies to bring key aspects of teaching English alive in your classroom.

We all work better when the conditions are right, so there is advice on setting the scene so that everyone knows what is expected of them, that it is OK to make mistakes and that learning is best when everyone is engaged. There are suggestions for behaviour for learning, the importance of knowing students as individuals and being enthusiastic about this important subject.

The underlying theme is that our students should be working harder than we are. So you will see that there are plenty of ideas which get them thinking, asking questions and reporting back. We need to be asking ourselves, 'What am I doing that a student could be doing?'

There is also advice on how to manage during inspection. Of course we want to show ourselves and our students at our best, but we need to remember that successful learning every day is what counts. Above all, let's remind ourselves of the pleasure of improving both our practice and our students' achievement day by day.

How to use this book

This book includes quick, easy, practical ideas for you to dip in and out of, in order to support you in teaching secondary English.

Each idea includes:

- A catchy title, easy to refer to and share with your colleagues.
- A quote from a teacher or student describing their experiences of the idea that follows or a problem they may have had that using the idea solves.
- A summary of the idea in bold, making it easy to flick through the book and identify an idea you want to use at a glance.
- A step-by-step guide to implementing the idea.

Each idea also includes one or more of the following:

Teaching tip	Taking it further	Bonus idea ★
Some extra advice on how or how not to run the activity or put the strategy into practice.	Ideas and advice for how to extend the idea or develop it further.	**There are 23 bonus ideas in this book that are extra exciting and extra original.**

Share how you use these ideas in the classroom and find out what other teachers have done using **#100ideas.**

Setting the Scene

Part 1

The physical space

"I always look forward to going to English lessons. The classroom is alive with great ideas."

Establishing a good physical environment for learning is important to send the right message to students. Outstanding English classrooms are full of images of great literature, students' work and prompts for thinking and writing and much more. It is important that your students know that they have stepped into an English classroom.

Teaching tip

Simple as it sounds, remember to change your displays and direct students' attention to key features, words and so on so that they know where to look for guidance or inspiration. Displays should not only look good; they need to be useful, too.

Make sure that the room you are teaching in is bursting with ideas and great stimuli for inspiring and focusing learning. Some ideas to get you started include:

- Print out quotes, laminate them and display them on the walls. Powerful quotes let students know that the classroom is a place of serious learning. They can also provide an introduction to texts and authors with which your students may be unfamiliar. Start with a few which resonate with you, but also get students to choose some and make them responsible for changing the quotes round the room on a regular basis. You can find some great quotes here: www.goodreads.com/quotes/tag/literature

- Select a poem or extract to display in a prominent place each half term or so. Select the work carefully – it could be thought provoking in terms of subject matter, challenging in terms of structure or language choices, use particular features of language especially well and so on. Students' eyes will often wander during lessons and having a piece of well-selected quality writing to alight upon can be useful. You can also use the piece of writing as a prompt to focus on key topics or aspects of writing.

- Students need to 'catch' a teacher's passion for the subject so make sure your classroom is filled with books that you know and love. This will make it easier for you to talk informally about what you liked or disliked about these books and how you decide what to read.
- Ask your students to research and create a display of different written forms from over the centuries, for example, pictographs, cuneiform signs, hieroglyphs, calligraphy, glyphs or runes. Similar projects could be undertaken for particular literary genres, authors or periods. Aim to provide frequent, purposeful opportunities for your students to get involved with text and see it as part of what they do in your lessons. The key to all of this is extending students' knowledge base so as to help provide a secure foundation for future learning.
- Display key features of language in your classroom. These may include, for example, rules for apostrophe use, spellings of irregular verbs, signposting language, speaking frames or sentence starters and so on. This can help establish the classroom as a place of learning and provide some ready prompts for students' own work.
- Get students to write mottos that represent the kind of atmosphere they expect to create and enjoy in their English lessons, and display them under the heading: 'The way things are done here'. Some examples might be: 'We listen to one another in our lessons'; 'We are committed to great learning in our English lessons'; 'We are open to new ideas'; 'We expect to make great progress'.

Taking it further

Get your students to help organise some of the displays in your English classroom. Teachers tend to think that they have to do everything, but giving students responsibility for aspects of classroom management can be a great way of increasing their commitment to the subject and giving them a sense of responsibility. What books do they most enjoy? How could they persuade someone else to read them? Arrange a rota including each class you teach, so they all get a go at being in charge of a display. Taking photos of the displays when they are up is a great way to keep a record of the work.

The listening classroom

"I don't want to be made to feel like a muppet!"

In order to help establish the conditions needed for great learning, everyone in the classroom needs to feel free to express their ideas without fear of ridicule. Use this activity to create an inclusive and safe environment in your classroom.

Always make your expectations explicit. In the classroom, everything should be up for discussion, as long as it is related to the topic and is conducted in a respectful way.

The psychological and social environment of the English classroom is as important as the physical environment. Practice is needed to fully develop these skills. Use the following activity to exemplify this to students:

- Divide the class into pairs of 'A' and 'B'. Student A has to talk for one minute on something they are interested in. Student B, having been primed by you, role-plays that they aren't listening.
- Ask the students to describe how it felt to be ignored and how they knew that student B was not listening to them. They are likely to come up with feelings such as angry, ignored, frustrated and lost for words.
- Ask students to decide what a good, active listener is and does.
- Repeat the exercise, but this time they must demonstrate active listening. Again, they should discuss how this felt. They are likely to say that they felt positive, that their ideas were worth listening to and that they were able to talk at more length than when they were ignored.
- To draw out the learning capture some of the responses. Students could create a poster that highlights what active listening is and why it should be a part of their classroom experience.

To reinforce the importance of respectful listening, ask students secondary questions based on what a fellow student has just said – not, as is often the case, 'What did Ishmael just say, Martin? Hmm? Hmm?' as punishment for not listening, but as part of your questioning approach in the classroom.

We were wondering . . .

"I expect my students to be continually thinking about what we are studying. One way of making sure they value this is to have a 'we were wondering' wall!"

English is jam-packed with wonderful opportunities for students to enjoy great language and literature, to think deeply, to speculate and to open up new horizons. Developing a 'we were wondering' wall is a great way of capturing some of their ideas.

We need to find ways to create an atmosphere in our classroom that shows that our students have a thirst for knowledge and love of learning. A quick and easy way of doing this is to have a regular supply of Post-it notes for students to jot down their ideas.

For example, when you are considering a new text for the first time, have the Post-it notes ready and ask students to make a note of anything they find interesting or puzzling. Some of these ideas will provide the trigger for discussion and learning within the lesson but there won't be enough time to consider others during the lesson and these could go on the www wall. However, only Post-its that will stimulate further thinking should go on the wall, and students need to know this. Until they can be trusted to use this sensibly, you reserve the right to remove any that are unsuitable.

Teaching tip

At a later date, take some of the examples from the wall and include them either as a small part of a lesson or as the focus for the main lesson objective. Building on students' responses and including their ideas in lesson planning makes the process organic, dynamic and affirms students' contributions.

Taking it further

Let students know that you will be using some of their ideas for future lessons. Select some Post-its that you think are particularly interesting or that may develop students' learning of a topic and allocate them to students to investigate. Expect them to feed back either to you or to the class as a whole. This can be light-touch (brief discussions) or extended into larger presentations.

Authentic audiences

"Too much of students' work ends up in an exercise book or folder. Who else might like to read or see their work?"

Think more imaginatively about the final destination for students' work. When we ask our students what happens to their work, they generally say that it goes into an exercise book or folder as revision for an exam. Whilst students' written work will have a theoretical intended audience and purpose, for some pieces of writing it may be useful to consider authentic audiences, too.

Taking it further

Keep a look out for issues either in the local community or on the internet that could be used as a stimulus for writing and framing an authentic response. Also, look at writing competitions, youth forums and other opportunities for your students to write something for an authentic outside audience.

This is not about finding an external destination for every scrap of work but certainly the longer pieces might be of interest to others. Start within the classroom - students can act as audiences for one another's work. This can be useful in terms of providing a model for good writing. It is important that you give students clear guidance about what good quality work looks like.

The next stage is to look beyond the classroom. Might another class be interested in the highlights of what has been produced? What about the head teacher, senior leaders and governors? People at home? How about an example for display in the entrance or English corridor?

Bonus idea ★

At the start of each unit, ask students to think about wider audiences for their work. Zoe Elder has written an excellent post on her blog about the shift in application and engagement when students are preparing their work for a discerning audience. www.fullonlearning.com/2014/02/01/creating-learning-events.

Engaging with reluctant learners

"Well, I have plenty of awkward customers in my groups – reluctant boys, chatty girls! I'm always on the lookout for new ideas to engage them."

In your classroom, it should be expected that all students will participate. This will, of course, mean utilising your knowledge of their needs and interests so as to plan learning that is appropriate, challenging and interesting.

One of the best ways of including the most reluctant students is to have high expectations that they will participate in the lesson, simply because the subject is so interesting. This may take some time, so don't give up! Here are a few ways of sparking initial engagement.

- Get them to make connections between their own interests and their study of English. Find out what other subjects they enjoy and ask them why. Do they think that they could incorporate some of the ideas from these other subjects into an English lesson? Let them know you are prepared to give it a try. Don't accept links which are trivial or time wasting!
- Tell them about your interests. Let them know what you are reading, why you are enjoying it or not and expect them to do the same. Let them see you reading!

Teaching tip

Students take their cue from us. If we are serious about our work, believe passionately in the subject and expect them to enjoy it then they will pick up on these messages. Take every opportunity to talk up your subject, the difference it has made to your life, its links to future employment and the sheer pleasure of enjoying a great book or having well developed language skills.

Know your students

"We all want to be acknowledged for the individuals we are. It is important to be noticed."

You may have lots of data on your class but you must remember that behind every piece of data is a human being. How can we get to know our students as individuals?

It is neither necessary nor appropriate to know every detail of your students' lives. However, knowing what their interests are, and some of the things they enjoy and worry about outside school, deepens relationships and can help improve their engagement and motivation.

When you first meet a group, set out your expectations for them as students and how you will be working together but also let them know that you want to get to know them as individuals. Ask them to complete the following statements:

One thing I really like is . . .

One thing I am really good at is . . .

In the future I hope to . . .

This exercise can pay dividends in terms of relationships. Providing students with this sort of exercise will make it clear that their voices will be heard and that this a place where everyone counts (including the teacher).

Behaviour for learning

"My students know what to expect in my classroom."

There is a focus on behaviour during inspections. This means there is more pressure than ever for classrooms to be orderly environments where everyone is expected to play their part. Inspections will consider the extent to which students' attitudes to learning help or hinder their progress in lessons. They will be looking for students' contribution to the culture of the school and their respect, courtesy and good manners towards each other and adults.

Classrooms are meant to be safe places where students want to be and where teachers enjoy working. An important part of this is that rules and expectations are made explicit early on. If you aren't managing the classroom, someone else will. Here are some ways of making this happen:

- Prior to starting a new job or placement, spend some time becoming wholly *au fait* with school policies, procedures and expectations. Knowing, for example, who Heads of Year are, what the school system for detention is or how sanctions and rewards are recorded, will help you feel and be more in control. It also makes it clear that you know what's what in the school – this is important!
- Make sure your students understand the systems and expectations that apply in your classroom. You will need to run through them with every new group. This will be a great investment of your time as it will help to ensure the calm and orderly atmosphere you want. Make sure you are persistent and you persevere even with the more tricky classes. Students need to be made aware that the classroom is a place of learning first and foremost and that you have high expectations of them all.

Teaching tip

Your knowledge and enthusiasm can be infectious. Let your students know how lucky they are to have the chance to study your subject and how much you enjoy teaching it. Tell them the story of how you came to teach the subject. Who inspired you? What books opened your mind to the magnificence of English? What was it like to study English at university? Share your struggles as well as your successes. This will help to inspire and motivate them to behave well in your classroom.

9

Beyond the English department

"I want to make sure I keep up to speed with national developments in my subject."

Boundary grade changes, reduction in controlled assessments, assessment of oral skills are just some of the factors which have had an impact on what and how we teach, so it's important to know where to look for the latest information.

Teaching tip

From 2015, increased focus on accurate spelling, punctuation and grammar will count for 20 per cent of the final exam in English Language which means that this will need to be a regular feature of classroom teaching. Although speaking and listening will not count towards the final marks they are still published. High quality speaking and listening informs the rest of students' learning and it is highly valued by employers, so again it is important that this element of teaching in English is maintained.

There are plenty of sources of information about the bigger educational picture for your subject. Your head of department will be in touch with the exam boards and they provide plenty of information on model answers and about the strengths and weaknesses of different parts of the exams.

There have been significant changes to GCSE. From 2014 the proportion of controlled assessment was cut and marks for the final written exams rose. As a result, for GCSE now, the final exam counts for 60 per cent and controlled assessment counts for 40 per cent. The coursework is made up entirely of reading and writing with no separate marks for oral skills. However, oral skills are still assessed but the results listed separately from the main English grade.

New GCSE English Language specifications come into effect for teaching from September 2015. This will be accredited through a final exam only. Ofqual (www.ofqual.gov.uk) has stated that this is to ensure consistency of standards and to free up time during lessons which had previously been taken up for controlled assessments. Students' speaking skills will be assessed but will not contribute to the overall grade. The assessment will be marked by teachers and reported separately, alongside the qualification grade on the certificate. 20 per cent of the marks for the written exams will be allocated to accurate spelling, punctuation and grammar.

English Literature will be assessed wholly by a final exam. Five per cent of the marks will be allocated to accurate spelling, punctuation and grammar.

The main difference between GCSE and iGCSE is that there was less coursework (which was optional) and more emphasis on the final exam. Schools have more flexibility over the range of books which they can choose to include for study. It is likely that iGCSE specifications on the coursework option will be brought in line with GCSE. As a result coursework is likely to be removed. At the time of going to press it appears that from 2017 the English iGCSE will not count in the league tables as they stand, which shows just how important it is to keep up with developments www.ofqual.gov.uk/news.

You can broaden your horizons if you link in with local networks of fellow specialists either through the local authority or academy group. Some of our most productive professional development comes from sharing ideas and talking shop with like-minded colleagues who are in the same field as you. It is also really important to belong to the professional association for English teachers: www.nate.org.uk which organises conferences, thought pieces from writers like Michael Rosen and great links from the Twitter feed on the homepage.

Taking it further

It is well worth subscribing to the news feed for Ofsted www.ofsted.gov.uk/news; Ofqual www.ofsted.gov.uk/news; the Department for Education www.gov.uk/government/announcements?departments[]=department-for-education as well as news sites such as the TES www.tes.co.uk/article.aspx?storyCode=6088067. You can touch base with the headlines briefly and this will be invaluable for helping you prioritise.

Beyond the scheme of work

"English is a treasure trove of beautiful literature, drama and poetry. Let's make sure we expose our students to as much of it as possible!"

There will always be a tension between covering a curriculum or programme of study and reading more widely. It is important that students are exposed to as many different types of literature as possible; experience of a variety of texts and the development of a reading culture are vital to developing students' language skills.

Use lessons after exams or towards the end of term as opportunities to dedicate time to giving students snapshots of the 'bigger picture' of English language texts. The idea here is to show the range and sweep of literature rather than attempting to do anything in depth. You are already doing this during the rest of your lessons, so these sessions are meant to provide exposure to other texts and reading habits. It is, of course, easy for this sort of exercise to be less than useful. Glassy-eyed students staring at a teen novel from the 80s is not what this should be about. Pick a play, maybe, and read it with the class. Try to make it something they are unlikely to study or select for themselves, for example, *The Importance of Being Earnest*.

Alternatively, ask studentes to choose books from the 'Writes of Passage' list compiled by the organisers of World Book Day: www. worldbookday.com/writes-of-passage. There are some great suggestions, including: *A Streetcar Named Bob*, *The Kite Runner*, *The Hitchhiker's Guide to the Galaxy* and *The Life of Pi*.

Challenge your students to read longer pieces of literature and difficult poems. Share your thoughts on difficult pieces and why you found them worth persevering.

Taking it further

A very amusing gallop through the history of English is available from the Open University: www.youtube.com/watch?v=rexKqvgPVuA. This will also stimulate ideas for more research for your students.

Or, read extracts from texts like Beowolf or The Canterbury Tales and then show students modern clips of the texts from YouTube:

Beowulf: www.youtube.com/watch?v=AJ_N3XH3ntl

Chaucer: www.youtube.com/watch?v=E3zUoNG_P_0

Preparing for Ofsted

Part 2

What happens during an Ofsted inspection?

"The prospect of an Ofsted inspection was so scary, but when it came to it, it felt like the inspector was focusing on the students, not on me!"

Being prepared for an Ofsted inspection will take some of the fear out of it. This idea will help as it gives an overview of what inspection teams are looking for.

The main purpose of an Ofsted inspection is to check how good the school's own evaluation is. If the school is saying that the quality of teaching is good then the inspection will take into account a number of indicators, including how much progress students make while at the school. As part of the inspection they will visit lessons across the school. They want to see as normal practice as possible. So, if you are doing a good job with your students day in and day out, it will show when your classroom is inspected. Inspectors will be able to observe that you expect everyone to be working hard, making a contribution and building on one another's answers. Students' books will show evidence of drafting and redrafting their work, and the feedback that they have used to improve their work. Your class displays will have examples of students' work, and will be designed to generate an ongoing love of language.

You are likely to have all this in place already, so while it is important to show your practice and your students at their best, there is no need to spend all night preparing a one-off lesson. If you do, your students are likely to be confused and the lesson may go less well than usual!

Ofsted, no quick tricks!

"Of course it's important to do well during an inspection, but we need to remember that we are running our lessons for students, not for Ofsted!"

Too much has been said about creating the perfect lesson for an inspection or formal observation. We need to move away from this because it doesn't give a true picture of our practice.

Inspections are there to check on the quality of teaching in a school, over time. So while the individual lesson counts, it only counts for so much. What is more important is the progress our students make in lessons over time. It is important to raise our game when we are being observed but not to spend all night preparing and putting on a special show. If you do, it will come across as false and experienced observers are able to spot this. Try to aim for good quality practice day in and day out – this will result in good or outstanding progress for your students over time.

What observers will be looking for is the impact of what you do on students' learning. So all that practice and work to get the behaviour for learning spot on and to show evidence of high quality feedback in books and through conversations throughout the lesson will pay off. But these are not quick fixes and they can't be put on for a show. So remind yourself and your groups that you are in this for the long term and the results will speak for themselves.

Teaching tip

It is a good idea to make as much of the learning as possible visible to the inspectors. Strategies such as 'think, pair share' will help with this. Regularly asking 'Why?' when students give a response and expecting others to do the same will show that conditions for progress are part of your everyday practice and you will get credit for that.

Ofsted myths!

"We are always trying to second-guess what Ofsted wants. This can't be a good idea!"

Ofsted produced a report 'Moving English Forward' in 2012 (www.ofsted.gov.uk/resources/moving-english-forward) which summarises the main strengths and areas for development in the subject. The report highlighted examples of good practice where students were not only making good progress but were also enjoying their lessons and it highlighted some of the most common myths surrounding what a good lesson looks like.

- The first myth relates to pace. The pace of the lesson needs to be appropriate to the lesson – faster does not always mean better learning. While we don't want to lose momentum, it is important not to race to keep to a tight timetable.
- The second myth is that teachers think that including more activities in a lesson will make it more effective. However, if students have too many activities they often can't finish them and learning is not consolidated or extended.
- Then there are myths about over-detailed and bureaucratic lesson plans and an inflexible approach to planning lessons. What happens here is that teachers sometimes feel that they should not depart from their plans during the lesson, even though students might need to move on more quickly or conversely, may more time on a particular activity.
- Inspectors also found that students were not given enough time to work independently – be it for reading, writing or to discuss issues. This is linked to a constant review of learning where students are expected to self- or peer-assess their work before they have completed more than a sentence or two.

Literacy across the curriculum

"Every teacher is a teacher of literacy."

Making literacy a focus across the curriculum will raise standards for all students. Whilst literacy is not the sole responsibility of teachers of English, colleagues will value the support that the English team can give them. The important thing is to suggest some approaches that may be useful within subject specific contexts rather than provide a bolt-on initiative that may not fit with subject content.

The important thing when it comes to literacy across the curriculum is for a school to have more than an agreed code for the marking of spelling, punctuation and grammar. Everyone in your school needs to have a wider view of literacy. Each subject uses language for particular purposes. What it mean to write like a scientist or read like an historian? What are the language skills most called upon within PE and Art? What kinds of talk, reading and writing are seen most frequently in history or geography?

One way of beginning to embed literacy across the curriculum is to encourage colleagues to make sure students have a secure grasp of the technical language and vocabulary related to their subject. Ensuring that students can use technical terms with confidence and understanding is really important. Ask colleagues to consider what types or reading and writing they most commonly engage with as part of their subject. Consider any ways in which these skills could be developed or supported though approaches used in English lessons, or in the other subjects themselves. For example, if students are expected to write evaluations or reports in science lessons, how can this be supported? If students are asked to skim or scan for key information in geography, what strategies may help with this? If students need to write instruction texts in DT, what are the features and language of those sorts of texts?

Teaching tip

There are good resources to support literacy across the curriculum: www. ofsted.gov.uk/resources/ moving-english-forward, www.learning.wales.gov. uk and www.sec-ed. co.uk/news/ofsted-calls-for-teachers-to-focus-on-literacy-across-all-subjects.

Taking it further

Students in every subject should be exposed to the language of that subject. Consider the approaches to teaching reading and writing or focusing and developing students' skills in speaking and listening that you use in your English lessons and how they may be used to inform the approaches of colleagues in other subjects.

Know your standards

"The Teachers' Standards are a useful reminder to keep my standards up and keep things simple!"

The Teachers' Standards have been in place since September 2012. They set out the expectations for teaching and personal and professional conduct.

'Teachers make the education of their pupils their first concern, and are accountable for achieving the highest possible standards in work and conduct. Teachers act with honesty and integrity; have strong subject knowledge, keep their knowledge and skills as teachers up-to-date and are self-critical; forge positive professional relationships; and work with parents in the best interests of their pupils.' (Teachers' Standards www.gov.uk/government/publications/teachers-standards.)

The following are some of the ways the Teaching Standards are relevant to an English teacher. They encourage teachers to:

- set high expectations which inspire, motivate and challenge students – at the heart of this is loving your subject, sharing with your class what English means to you and referring regularly to great poets, dramatists and novelists.
- promote good progress and outcomes by students – you must know about your students' abilities, particularly in the vulnerable groups, and convey to them that everyone can succeed if they put their minds to it.
- demonstrate good subject and curriculum knowledge – keep your own learning near the top of the agenda. Make sure you always have a great novel on the go and skim the blogs and Twitter accounts of some great English teachers who will give you the

headlines of the latest thinking in the subject, for example, @HuntingEnglish, @geoffbarton, @LearningSpy, @joe__kirby, @atharby.

- plan and teach well-structured lessons – think 'big picture' first and focus primarily on what you want your students to learn as opposed to what you want them to do in your lesson.
- adapt teaching methods to respond to the strengths and needs of all students – allow flexibility in your planning, make the learning visible, check what they already know and provide appropriate challenge for all students.
- make accurate and productive use of assessment – know your students' prior attainment, use selective information to tell a big story and don't fall into the trap of marking every piece of work.
- manage behaviour effectively to ensure a good and safe learning environment – everyone has the right to learn and you have the right to teach. Students need regular reminders about the importance of your classroom being a great place for talking, thinking and learning.
- fulfil wider professional responsibilities – be prepared to get involved in wider school activities, collaborate with your colleagues, take responsibility for your own continuing professional development and treat parents as allies!

Taking it further

Have these standards in mind as you go about your work. To keep them fresh take one each term and really think through how you could become an expert practitioner in this respect. For example, one school I know of decided to improve the gaps in attainment for particular groups through conducting student surveys. The findings were used to adjust schemes the following term.

Every student on track

"Using data to ensure everyone makes progress is vital."

Handling huge quantities of data may feel daunting, but many schools have strategies in place to help manage it. For example, some are producing helpful grids or using specific software systems to show where the level of students' learning starts and where they might reasonably be expected to be by a certain year.

Teaching tip

It is, of course, important to remember that data does not provide the whole picture – one student's Level 4 in reading may be quite different form another's, and each child may require quite different approaches and next steps.

Schools are held to account for the difference they make to the lives of young people. So the question we need to ask is: How much value are we adding to students' knowledge skills and understanding? Ask for data support and training from your school if you need it. You need to know the following headlines:

- Key Stage 2 SATS scores in English and maths
- CAT scores
- SEN, Pupil Premium, G&T
- Where your students should be by the end of the term, year and Key Stage.

Use a colour-coding system to show whether students are making more than expected progress, expected progress or less than expected progress. If you have photos of students on your system you can highlight the photos with different coloured frames; for students who are not making progress, their colour frame will be red, if they are progressing as expected, the frame will be amber and if it is above the expected level it will be green.

You need to let the reds know that they are under-performing. There may be legitimate reasons (not the same as excuses) for this, but many need to know that they need to raise their game. Similarly, the amber group need to know that they must to keep working as hard as they are. And you need to be considering how the green group can be challenged.

Why are they doing it?

"I sometimes feel that I spend too much time planning elaborate resources when I should be concentrating on what I want my students to learn."

There are many ways to organise lessons and they do not necessarily have to come in distinct phases, have the same structure each time or involve a myriad of different approaches and a flurry of stickers. What they should do is focus on developing students' skills, knowledge or understanding. In short there should be some learning rather than just lots of doing.

Below are some strategies you should employ for every lesson to ensure students are learning.

- Consider what it is that your students will have gained by being in your lesson. What is it that they now know, understand, can do or maybe do better, that they couldn't before?
- Whether or not you share the learning objective with your students at the start, or get them to write it in a book, is a matter of choice and debate. What is important, though, is that you yourself have a very clear idea of what the aim of the lesson is and how you are going to know whether it has been achieved.
- Refer back to your learning objective at key points in your lesson. This will help you, and your students, see what progress is being made.
- Have success criteria: think about how you will know your students have met your learning objective. Will this be incremental? Will it come at the end?
- Task setting should be purposeful. Tasks should be about learning rather than simply engaging or keeping students occupied for a period of time. Think about what you want them to learn by the end of the lesson and after each task ask whether it helps them get there.

Teaching tip

At the end of each task try saying 'You have just (for example, identified some descriptive language in this passage) and now you are going to use that to (for example, change this next passage into one with a quite different atmosphere).' If you can't make this type of statement, it may well be that the students are doing 'stuff' but not working towards an appropriately challenging aim for the lesson. This is not necessarily true of every lesson, of course, but, as a general tip to help keep focus, it is useful.

Making marking manageable

"Who hasn't struggled under a mountain of marking? But help is at hand ..."

We need to be very clear about our rationale for marking. It is not realistic or effective to mark every piece of work a student produces. Nonetheless, you need to know how your students are progressing and they need to know that their work will be looked at. The marking should reflect the school's feedback and marking policy. It is helpful to prioritise feedback over marking.

Teaching tip

There are some very good ideas to make marking and data collection manageable from Andy Tharby where he describes how he provides 'rolling, live feedback' http://reflectingenglish.wordpress.com/2014/04/18/a-second-bite-at-the-cherry-thoughts-on-redrafting-writing/

What is the difference between marking and feedback? Marking shows that the work has been checked for accuracy. Feedback provides suggestions for moving the learning forward. What is often seen in books during an inspection is that teachers give good feedback but the students have not responded. Why not? This is usually down to time, as we rush on to the next piece of work, but it can be a wasted opportunity for students to improve their work. They should be spending at least the same amount of time developing their work as the teacher has spent giving them the feedback. If the feedback was worth writing, it deserves the students' attention. A helpful way of thinking about this is to view feedback as an ongoing conversation about learning.

To make marking manageable, decide that you are only going to give feedback on certain pieces of work. Ideally, this feedback should be focused on one of the drafts for an extended piece. The expectation is that students will incorporate the comments into the final piece and respond to the teacher's comments to show how they have taken them on board. The idea here is that drafting and redrafting are important.

This is what a manageable feedback workflow might look like:

- Set expectations with students that you will be giving detailed feedback at certain points and that you expect them to respond and improve their work.
- Skim work during lessons so that you can identify common themes which have either been misunderstood or not been developed enough. These do not need to be individually marked, but fed into your planning. As a starter, or during the lesson, go through any such misunderstandings as a whole class or a small group. Get students to use a different coloured pen and write down what improvement is needed and how they will change their work. This can also be applied to common misspellings. What is important here is that the feedback is acted on in the classroom and the use of a different coloured pen signals that feedback has been given and received.
- For the more detailed feedback on students' work, it is helpful to give feedback in the form of questions, for example, 'Can you given another example which shows this? Where else have you come across this feature? Give reasons for your answer.' Expect students to act on it!

Taking it further

To show your classes 'how we do business here' make your feedback principles evident through wall displays and in students' books and folders.

Visualise it!

"Using a visualiser has made an incredible difference to my teaching practice."

A visualiser is a fixed camera, like a webcam, that is connected to a whiteboard and allows you to show work to the whole class through the large screen. When used well, it can make a lesson really interactive. The best thing about a visualiser is its flexibility: it can be used to show a close-up technique that would otherwise be difficult to show to the whole class.

Taking it further

Use the visualiser to show examples of outstanding pieces of work, either from the class or from other groups. This helps raise everyone's game!

Bonus idea ★

Use this clip 'Austin's Butterfly' www.vimeo.com/38247060 and ask the students to formulate their own ideas about how to give feedback which is specific, constructive and kind.

Here are some effective ways to use a visualiser:

- To share a poem or piece of prose with the class. It saves photocopying time and allows you to use resources as quickly as you come across them. You can use a highlighter for the key points or ask students to point out which elements they think are most interesting. This way of working encourages speculative talk which develops students' writing.
- To show an object or artefact as a stimulus for writing. It means everyone has the chance to see the object at the same time. Again, this opens up conversations and speculation about what is seen.
- To help with drafting. Include your own work along with a selection of students' work in progress and discuss as a group the parts that are strong and if there any areas that could be improved. This creates a real sense of immediacy and agency during the lesson.

Get on Twitter!

"Twitter is the best way to get top-notch professional development. There are so many great ideas being shared every day!"

Twitter can be daunting for anyone who has not used it. However, there are plenty of people and tools out there to help you.

There are Twitter evangelists and there are sceptics. Here are some of the things people who use Twitter are saying:

'It's great to be able to ask questions and get answers from other professionals. It saves hours of time.'

'It takes me beyond the school and it means I bring great ideas to meetings and to my classroom.'

There are some terrific sites to help you get going. A great site is 'Bring a Teacher to Twitter': www.batttuk.wordpress.com, which will guide you through setting up an account. And sites like www.ictevangelist.com will help you to find plenty of links to take you further. You don't have to join Twitter, you can look at ideas and links and follow conversations from the sidelines, but you will get so much more out of it if set up your own account and get involved – ask questions, retweet interesting ideas and share your ideas. You will be amazed at how quickly any questions get answered!

Taking it further

Why not set up a Twitter account for your students to contribute to? It is possible to protect accounts so that they are only available to people agreed by you. There are plenty of ways that Twitter can be used to extend learning; for example, 50 suggestions can be found here: www. teachhub.com/50-ways- use-twitter-classroom.

Blog!

"Setting up a blog seemed like another piece of work to begin with. But I soon realised it is a great way of sharing ideas and key pieces of work."

There are several uses for blogs — some teachers use them to write their own thoughts about teaching and learning and others set up class blogs to use with their students.

If you are considering writing your own blog about your teaching, first take a look at some of the teachers who are sharing their thoughts. You will notice that they do not talk about individual students or colleagues. They discuss new ideas they are trying or issues which arise in learning. Blog entries of about 500 to 700 words are the most effective as they can be scanned quickly. You will find that very few boast about their practice but rather put their ideas out for others to comment on and refine. To set up a blog, sites such a Wordpress are free and have a good range of templates to choose from.

To create a class blog, you could replace the classic 'write a newspaper report' with 'write a blog'. This takes students' work to a wider audience as it can appear on the school's website and helps them to embed their ICT skills.

Taking it further

Ask students to research blogs that reflect their interests outside school. These could be related to sports or hobbies or current affairs. Encourage them to analyse why these are useful to readers. What can they learn that would be useful for a class blog? Examples of class blogs from around the world can be found at www.theedublogger. com/check-out-these-class-blogs and at www.freetech4teachers. com/2013/08/40-examples-of-classroom-school-blogs.html.

Speaking and Listening

Part 3

The importance of talk

"The ability to have our ideas heard is one of our deepest human needs."

Students' skills in oracy are often underdeveloped — they can already talk, (sometimes it seems it is all they do!) so why does it need to be taught? Much student talk, however, is social. Developing their academic talk is not just a benefit in itself, but can also result in better quality written work.

Speaking and listening are not, in practice, discrete curricular elements, easily separated from reading or writing. Frequently, these strands are found in the same lesson as skills in one area inform those in another. Student talk is often something they 'do' rather than something that is actively developed. This is a missed opportunity. Think about how to best extend and develop the speaking skills of your students. Rather than simply instructing them to 'discuss', for example, put in place a clear purpose and structure for their talk.

Speaking and listening, much like writing, will have a particular focus, audience and purpose. Speaking frames can provide useful prompts that help focus students' talk and move it from the social to the academic. It can also help students to bridge the gap between their spoken language and their writing. Display and provide students with words and phrases that they can use to structure their talk. These may include:

This suggests . . .

On the other hand . . .

I disagree because . . .

I have changed my mind because . . .

My thinking was different because . . .

Lost in the jungle!

"When we put our students in fictional challenging circumstances they are surprisingly inventive in coming up with ideas for survival."

This type of exercise is effective as an assessment of skills of group work, persuasion, problem-solving and decision-making.

Put students into groups of four and present them with a background story, for example:

Their group has been on a plane which has crash-landed in the rainforest. Their small plane is wrecked and cannot be repaired. They do not know how long they will be lost, or the location of the nearest town or village.

Present students with a list of items that they can take on their journey. Each group selects a number of items but they can only take items up to a certain weight limit (for example, 28 weight units) and must, therefore, think carefully about their decisions. For example:

☐ 3 × blankets	4 weight units each
☐ 1 × flare gun	3 weight units
☐ 1 × box of waterproof matches	1 weight unit
☐ 1 × 6ft square tarpaulin	3 weight units
☐ 5 × 5ltr water containers (full)	5 weight units each
☐ 3 × machetes	3 weight units each
☐ 1 × 12ft rope	4 weight units
☐ 100 × painkilling tablets	1 weight unit
☐ 1 × gas camp stove (full)	2 weight units
☐ 1 × book 'Edible Plants'	2 weight units
	28 units

Monitor each group as they make their selections. Then ask each group to present their choices to the class, giving reasons for their decisions. Extend this activity by giving the groups another problem to solve using just those items that they have chosen to take with them, for example, a group member has a broken leg, or they must cross a river.

Teaching tip

Ask students to explain *how* they made their decisions. This is different from saying *what* they did and will help them to articulate their decision-making, for example, how they went about resolving disagreements and made compromises. Explain to them that talking about learning and collaborating will help them apply these skills in other lessons.

Speaking in public

"For me, the thought of giving a talk on my own was scary. But after we talked about how everyone feels nervous beforehand I felt more confident about giving it a go."

The ability to present their own ideas to a group in a coherent and interesting way is one that is both personally satisfying for students and a vital skill for school and beyond.

Teaching tip

Remind students that they are being assessed on their talk and make sure they are familiar with the expectations. Students often write a great speech, but the specifics of speaking and listening assessment need to be made clear.

The individual student talk is one of the more daunting aspects of English lessons for some students. For others, it is a marvellous opportunity to let the world know about their love of Manchester United or fishing. That said, even when they are talking about a personal interest, it is still necessary to teach students the specific skills to ensure that their talk has focus and engages their audience. Just as in writing, the purpose and audience of the talk provides the focus and, hence, the language, tone, and so on. The skills will be different for different types of talk.

The individual extended talk can be quite a challenge as a teacher. It is exceptionally time consuming; students (and teachers) seem to lose their ability to focus after the fifth talk and often the purpose is unclear. It is sometimes not well supported. Students simply go off and research a topic and then deliver a talk on it. Clear guidance and focus is needed in developing students' speaking and listening. Just as with a piece of writing, make sure students consider:

- Audience and purpose —make these explicit because the structure, time and language stems from there.
- Timing — be sure that students have a set time for their talk and stick to it.
- Language choice and devices —once audience and purpose have been decided,

develop students' understanding of how to best structure their talk and what language and devices they should consider. Remind them their talk is the end point of a series of lessons.

- Presentational skills –think about gesture, body language, expression and intonation, facial expression and so on.

Before students embark on planning their talks, show them examples of effective speeches and identify some of the features that make them compelling. Depending on the focus of the task, you may want to show them how to include: rhetorical questions (ones that do not need an answer because it is self evident); repetition in order to make a point; lists of three which make the same point in different ways; contrast such as 'on the one hand, but on the other'; emotive language; direct address such as 'I'm sure you'll agree with me'; evidence, for example, statistics, quotations, examples; or, depending on topic and focus, humour and engagement with the listening audience.

However well prepared students are, some will be battling with their nerves. Teach your students the following ways to overcome their nerves:

- Having written out their talk and familiarised themselves with its content, they can prepare small cards with key points of the speech. These points will help them to keep to their structure.
- Practise several times, preferably in front of a listening audience.

Taking it further

Try to provide students with a challenge in their speaking and listening tasks, rather than simply a 'talk' on a topic of their choice to an unspecified audience. Give them a focus that will mean they have to really consider their choices.

Bonus idea ★

Prepare your own individual talk about a topic of interest to you. You can use this to model good practice or you can use it to show what a weak individual talk looks like. Students can then revise and improve this in terms of content, language skills and delivery. This can act an effective shared modelling exercise.

Developing questioning

"I got much better quality responses when I started to focus on how to use questioning with my groups."

Too often we expect our students to give quick responses to our questions. Then, when they don't reply immediately, we can be tempted to answer the question ourselves. Thinking about how to develop your questioning skills and the reasons why you are using questions in the classroom can reap benefits.

Questioning in the classroom has many purposes: to check understanding, to encourage students to explore ideas and make connections about a text, or to explain a point of view. Questioning is not a simple hierarchy with knowledge-based questions at the bottom; rather, questions are used for a variety of learning purposes, some of which might well be to check knowledge (which itself can be complex).

Think carefully about the questions you ask your class. If questions are to be used to explore key ideas or to check vital information has been understood, it may make sense to plan your questions. It may also help to consider what you want to get out of the questions.

In order to encourage more developed responses from students and in turn help develop their speaking and listening skills, the following may be useful:

- Use a variety of questions for different learning purposes. Use secondary questions in a focused way so as to generate discussion and encourage students to provide more developed responses. This also models good listening for students.
- When exploring ideas through questions, encourage students to build upon and

develop one another's responses. This will need to be structured by you, initially at least. You can use sets of speaking frame cards to help structure responses.

- Use strategies such as 'Think, Pair, Share': students are given a little time to consider a question and come up with an initial response which is then shared with a partner and discussed and developed further. Important to this process is that students are given the tools for discussion. Be aware that, without preparation, this may not produce anything more than two students who know as little as one another sharing their misconceptions. When prepared for with a clear purpose, however, it can be very effective.

Some key questions need to be asked at set points in the lesson so as to check understanding. Mini-whiteboards or even just pieces of paper are an easy way to collect this sort of snapshot information from the whole class. Make sure the question is clear and that it is focused on collecting an overview of understanding at that point in the lesson. The question should give students simple choices -option A, B, C or D. Students write their chosen option on their whiteboard and hold it up to you. This should be quick and conducted with the minimum of fuss, so make sure you are prepared.

Get students to ask their own questions. This could be related to a text they are studying or a type of writing they are working towards. Get them to produce questions that may provide some further insight into an event or a language choice. These can be answered by you, the class or another student. You could put them on your 'we were wondering' wall (see idea 3) and select a few to focus some group work the next lesson. Or provide a series of answers and ask students to devise the question that would have produced that answer.

Story sharing

"After nourishment, shelter and companionship, stories are the thing we need most in the world." Phillip Pullman

This is a short and sweet activity that tests students' listening skills and their ability to engage an audience.

Teaching tip

You can use this activity to develop some 'ingredients' for effective engagement in speaking and in writing. You can focus equally on both the language choice made and the presentational elements, such as body language and voice. You could also show them examples of great storytellers on TED, www.ted.com/themes/master_storytellers.html.

Tell students a story – this may be about yourself or something fictional. Initially, present it in a flat and uninteresting way. Elicit their thoughts about how you could make the story more interesting for an audience. Retell your story using the suggested improvements and ask students to collect ideas about what worked and what didn't. Record these on the board. Ask students to tell a partner a story about themselves. This can fit in as part of a wider sequence of lessons based around autobiography or horror stories, for example. Students then take turns to retell their partner's story using the agreed suggestions to make it as interesting as they can. Give clear time guidelines to this activity, as some students will squash their story into two or three sentences, while others could happily fill the entire lesson up.

The proposal

"A proposal can be seen from a number of points of view. I found it interesting to hear what other groups had to say about how the proposal would affect them."

This exercise gives students the chance to look at a proposal from several different perspectives. If possible, use an example that is relevant to the school's local community.

Ideally, this group task will need a couple of lessons to be really effective. Set a scenario for the class such as one of the following:

An improvement grant has been awarded to the local community and various groups are invited to submit bids.

or

A new supermarket is to be built in the local area and groups are invited to submit their views regarding location and suitability.

Split the class into interest groups of four or five. Depending on the scenario you choose, these could include teenagers, pensioners, environmentalists, parents and so on. Vary the scenario and group identities to suit your class.

Each group presents their proposal to the class. This should also include reasons why the proposals put by the other groups are less appealing. Key to this sort of task is that students use the language of persuasion to present their proposal as effectively as possible.

Teaching tip

Ask students to make links between this work and other subjects in the curriculum, for example, geography, which often considers proposals for new developments and the impact they might have on different groups.

Taking it further

This task can be embellished by devising extra resources to support the proposal, for example, a map that identifies significant features such as preservation sites, local schools and hospitals. Students can also be encouraged to consider the points that will be raised by other interest groups and come up with convincing rebuttals.

Great debates!

"Be bold, don't back down, know your arguments!"

Debate can be used to assess students' work in pairs or individually. It is important that students know the rules governing debate so that they can take part maturely. It is also important that they have been given the opportunity to develop the language skills required in preparation for this sort of task.

First, introduce the notion of debate as distinct from argument. Then give students a set of simplified rules and explain that these will govern the debates:

a) The idea of a motion in the form 'This house believes that . . .'
b) The roles of the people to be involved, which should include chair, proposer of motion and opposer of motion.
c) Strict time constraints, after which each speech must end. This can be altered depending on the class, but try not to make it too long.
d) The role of the audience as observer, not participator. This rule can be relaxed to include an organised question-and-answer session after the debate if you wish.
e) Outlines regarding the form of each speech such as making the case, anticipating counter arguments, coming to a conclusion.
f) A standard format for the debates, for example, chair introduces the motion and each speaker; proposer's speech; opposer's speech; summing up by chair.

For their first debate, give students the motion to be debated and decide whether they will be proposing or opposing. If necessary, you can also act as chair so as to ensure that the debates run smoothly.

Balloon debate

"I told the students that two people must be thrown from a leaking hot air balloon to keep it airborne or everyone on board will die – that concentrated the mind!"

A balloon debate hinges around persuading others that your role is more important to humanity than others. In justifying their place in a hot air balloon, students are using and developing their skills for making persuasive arguments.

Divide the class into groups of six to eight. One member of each group should be an observer taking notes on how persuasive each student is, making sure individuals in the group are listening to one another, monitoring that they keep to the point and that they do not get too emotional! Your own monitoring skills will be called upon here, too.

Assign each of the other students a character, for example, nurse, airline pilot, farmer, scientist, schoolteacher, and politician. Each of these students represents one member of a group of people in a hot air balloon that is too heavy and must lose some of its passengers. Each person must argue, in character, why they should be saved. Give the groups enough time to identify the key aspects of each role and think through the contribution which their character makes to humanity. They need to remember that if they are thrown overboard their contribution to humanity goes with them.

Take it in turns for each group to go through the debate. The other groups as audience evaluate the relative cases and vote the people off the balloon one by one. After each group has taken its turn, ask the observers to comment on how each group decided who should stay and the most impressive examples of persuasion.

Teaching tip

Remind students that although it can be hard to reach a consensus, they should try their best to encourage everyone to buy into the eventual solutions. They should view differences of opinion as opportunities for creative discussion. Encourage them not to reach a conclusion before all the options have been fully aired. Each group can also be asked to select the one character they would save. The groups can then listen to each of these balloon 'champions' and select their final survivor!

Building on answers

"When I was expected to build on other people's answers it made me concentrate more on what they were saying as well as my own thoughts. It meant my ideas were even better."

Debates, dialogues and discussions are very useful tools in the classroom. As well as extending and developing students' speaking and listening skills, they are an opportunity to explore ideas and opinions and to practise and enhance skills of reasoning and working with others.

Giving students the structure to create more complex and interesting responses will develop their thinking and their reasoning. One way of doing this is to give them an ABC framework for building on answers:

A = agree with; B = build upon and C = challenge

These can be given out as cards so that students know that they either have to agree with, build upon or challenge. When they have had practice at this encourage them to use the A,B and C strategies whenever you have a class discussion.

For more information on how to use this go to: www.huntingenglish. com/2013/12/26/ disciplined-discussion-easy-abc.

Present to your students a scenario based upon a disagreement, for example, parents/guardians forbidding their child from attending a party. Split the class into two and ask one half to jot down what they think the parents' objections might be, and the other to jot down the reasons the child may have for being allowed to go. As students feed back to the class, note their comments on the board.

Next ask students in pairs or small groups to see if there are links between any of the comments or if there any comments that they feel answer each other/cancel each other out. Ask them also to identify any common areas of concern – for example, missing out on a meeting with friends. Students then feed back to the class, indicating where they feel an objection has been met with a valid reason. If the class agrees, that objection is crossed out. Similarly, if there is an area of common ground, this should be highlighted. Students will hopefully see that, often, differences of opinion do share common ground and also that some agreement can be reached through consideration of another's point of view.

Reading

Part 4

Reading for meaning

"Reading for understanding is one of the most important skills for our students. They need to read beyond the surface and unpick what the writing is trying to convey."

Use a range of questions to improve students' skills in reading for meaning. Being able to identify the key points of a text as well as the underlying meaning and the writer's craft is an essential skill, not only to improve their enjoyment of a text but for exam success. It will also improve their own writing.

Students complete numerous comprehension exercises during their time in school, both in class and at each end of Key Stage examination. Tasks that help students with their writing, for example, adjective use or creating atmosphere, introduce the skills that students will need to use when analysing texts, so make that link clear.

Some comprehension questions are 'what' questions, which ask students to retrieve information. These will generally be lower-tariff questions in exams, so remind students not to spend too long on their answers. Higher-tariff questions will ask students to comment on the 'how' of a piece of writing. They generally require students to comment on how a particular atmosphere is created, or how a character is feeling. To answer these 'how' questions effectively, students need to be trained to look for 'clues' in text.

Give students a glossary of literary techniques and devices including, for example: alliteration, figurative language, characterisation, suspense, humour, irony. While terminology alone won't gain students marks, it does act as a good shorthand when they write about text and makes their writing seem more sophisticated. However, most important is that students can identify and discuss *how* text works.

Taking it further

Ask students to work in pairs to become 'experts' in one aspect of the literary devices described in the main idea. They must be able to explain what these are, how they work and provide examples to help other students improve their work. When we expect students to know and understand something in depth so that they can explain it to others, they take on new information more quickly. It is important however, not to simply reduce texts to a list of devices, and to ensure the key focus is kept on the impact of that text and how that was created.

Reading for clues

"Students enjoy looking for clues. When they read a text, they begin to ask 'What else might be going on here?'"

Breaking down big pieces of writing into smaller chunks not only makes things easier to tackle but also allows students to go into greater depth.

Teaching tip

For the first few sections, at least, ask students to stop after each section and share their answers so as to ensure that all are on the right track. Some students' answers will be more detailed than others. They can be asked to go a stage further and analyse why the 'clue words' led them to their conclusion.

Rather than give students a whole extract to analyse, give them a piece of text that has been broken into short chunks with no more than three questions on each section. You can use any text you feel is suitable or, to make sure that the devices are readily accessible to students, you could write your own.

One way to introduce the idea is to base the text around a mystery or treasure hunt, with textual clues to be picked up throughout. This can help reinforce the idea of a 'search' rather than a cursory reading. For example:

Jason folded the piece of paper as small as he could and stuffed it in the secret compartment in the heel of his boot. He glanced down at its previous owner, still and white. 'Funny how they always look so peaceful afterwards,' he thought. Pausing for a moment, he washed his hands, put on some of the man's cologne and quietly closed the door.

Taking it further

Ask students to work in pairs to create their own short text with clues. Working this way takes the pressure off an individual having to do all the work on their own and will generate more ideas. Students exchange their pieces and compare the range of clues others came up with. Encourage them to look for clues in any piece of writing they come across.

What has Jason just done? What made you think this?

Has he done this before? What made you think this?

Why do you think he did it? What made you think this?

Continue in the same vein, setting questions after small sections of text that encourage students to look for 'clues'.

Extracting meaning

"Demonstrating analytical skills is central to getting those higher grades."

While many students realise the importance of knowing and understanding, they also need to develop the skills of analysis. Not only does this take them deeper into the text, it also gives them important wider skills for other subjects, such as reading for bias in history.

Use an extract to focus on the specifics of a high-tariff question in an exam. Ask students to look closely at the question and any bullet points that may have been given as guidance, and to underline key words. They will use these words to structure their answer and the bullet points serve as paragraph headings.

Students could also make tables with headings such as 'device/ language/ structure', 'effect created' and 'what x does' or 'what this shows us'.

The formula for structured responses of this kind has many names, for example, PEE – Point, Evidence, Explanation; SEC – Statement, Evidence, Comment. They follow the same basic format:

I think that Jason has killed someone before [point]. I think this because he says 'they always look so peaceful' [evidence]. The word 'they' suggests there has been more than one and 'always' also suggests that he has seen more than one dead body. [explanation]

These formulas are a good starting point to get students into the habit of justifying and explaining their answers. However, in a long answer the formula can become very repetitive and can limit some responses, so provide students with a variety of phrases that they can use in their writing to avoid repetition.

Developing deduction

"We act like sleuths to work out what is really going on. Great fun!"

Deduction is one of the most important skills we can help our students to develop. It involves deeper thinking, speculation and sharing ideas with others. The great thing is that students really enjoy doing this because they are naturally curious.

Teaching tip

Ask students to make a summary of the processes at work in deduction. Explaining how to use clues to tell a big story means they can then transfer these skills when they read texts. Encourage them to talk through their thought processes.

As English teachers, we encourage our students to read for clues and to be able to infer, deduce and understand connotation. Tasks such as these enhance our students' reading, writing and thinking skills. The following task and its variants are best organised as group or paired activities, as discussion and debate are important aspects in terms of outcome and process. You can choose to use these activities over several lessons. The number of lessons needed will depend on your intended outcome and the needs of the class.

Prepare an image of a flat or house. You can use collage, ICT, sketching or any other method available to you, although an IWB is probably the most flexible. Display or distribute the image to the class. Tell them that the property has been found empty and that, as investigators, they have to find out as much as possible about the occupant and where they may have gone. Be sure to provide sufficient detail for the students – torn curtains, pristine hedges, ornate door furniture, bars over the windows or a child's toy hanging up. Ask students to note down their thoughts about the occupants. They then feed back to class, giving reasons for their deductions.

Next, display or distribute a picture or series of pictures of the interior of the property. Again, provide potential clues in your images – a torn calendar, a space where a picture might have been, bookcases filled with carefully selected texts, a home gym, photographs, car keys on a bedside table and so on. Ask students to develop their investigation in the light of their new findings and report back to the class with their deductions regarding the occupants and where they may now be. A number of tasks can be set at this point – ask your students to draw character profiles of the occupant/s and use these, alongside their deductions; to write a narrative leading up to the point at which the property was vacated; a report about their findings; a series of questions to ask other groups so as to come to an agreed set of events or a newspaper story, among other options. You can, of course, differentiate this task fairly easily simply by varying the types and number of clues you leave.

Taking it further

Students can share their ideas and use their questioning skills to probe one another's findings. They can then decide upon the most plausible ideas, giving reasons for their answers and explaining if they had their mind changed by anyone else's ideas.

Bonus idea ★

Take a short story and stop after the first page and ask students to make some guesses about what might happen next. Capture these either on Post-its on a visualiser and refer to them as the story progresses. It doesn't matter if they don't get all the answers right, it is the process of looking for clues which is important.

More on deduction

"Hmm, what can we tell from these clues?"

Asking students to use their newly developed deduction skills in their own work will give them the chance to let their imaginations run wild, within reason!

Bring into class a ready-prepared bag of shopping and tell the students it has been found in a specific location, for example, on a bus, at an ice-skating rink, in a nightclub or in a phone box.

Explain to students that they are investigators and must paint as full a picture as possible of the person who has left this bag behind, based on its contents and the location in which it was found. Similarly, present to the class several items that have been found in a bin or in a car. Include items such as receipts, hair clips, torn envelopes, travel tickets and so on. These tasks can be combined to make an extended activity over a series of lessons with further additions from you – a tape recording of a phone message, or an item of clothing.

Once students have completed their investigations they could present their findings to the class as a speaking and listening assessment, or write up their accounts as a formal report, a narrative or a play script. Alternatively, they could produce a news programme or write up their findings on a class blog.

Comprehension

Part 5

Making assumptions

"Begin challenging your own assumptions. Your assumptions are your windows on the world. Scrub them off every once in a while, or the light won't come in." Alan Alda

Working with students to spot assumptions helps them to read texts with fresh eyes. Make sure they are clear about what is meant by 'assumption' — that it is something that is taken for granted. Assumptions are not necessarily a bad thing; they are important to recognise because they can have an impact on the arguments being made.

Taking it further

Make this task more sophisticated by asking students to choose between assumptions that appear to be similar. For example, using 'Romeo and Juliet' this may include: people should stand up for what they feel, no matter what the consequences; people should take consequences into account in order to make the best decision; people should learn how to play the system to get what they want, and so on. Working in this way is helpful for leading into debates about ethics as well as encouraging students to develop questioning skills.

Give students a short piece of text. This may be from a newspaper article or a piece of literature in which you can identify a list of assumptions. It is important that a set of fairly clear assumptions can be drawn from the piece. For example, if you chose an extract from 'Romeo and Juliet', list assumptions underneath such as: young people don't think before they act; love is the most powerful emotion; secrets have bad consequences and so on.

Students then discuss the assumption they find most interesting as a class or in groups. The class agrees which, if any, of the assumptions they feel are less problematic. This sort of task invites students to examine what they know about a given text, while also thinking about what assumptions are, how we reach them, whether they have any value, how they can be examined, and so on.

Comparing and contrasting

"Learning to compare themes and contrasts meant we got new insights into what we were reading."

We often ask students to 'compare and contrast' in the English classroom, and we usually take it for granted that they can do this but often students are simply listing differences, which is not quite the same thing. Being able to make connections between ideas, texts or objects is an important skill.

Display two quite different objects, for example, a board pen and a book. Ask students to list similarities and differences. A Venn diagram or a table could be used to present the findings. Next, show students two or more objects that are similar in some ways but quite different in others – an apple and a tennis ball, for example. Discuss the differences and ask the class to categorise them into types of difference and similarity, including, for example, appearance, feel and function.

Students then complete a diagram or list to see if objects are more alike than unalike, based on different criteria. Students decide in pairs which comparison criteria they think is most important, why and if this is the case in all instances. Students may decide, for instance, that while a tennis ball might *look* more like an apple than a pineapple does, the pineapple is actually more similar to the apple as they are both fruit. Be sure that your students are equipped with the vocabulary of comparison: the same, similar, but, because, however, unlike and so on.

These skills are then applied to text. Give your students an information text about species of dog or British theme parks for example, and ask them to compare and contrast the types described within. Alternatively, give the class two texts (fiction or non-fiction) to compare.

Teaching tip

Ask students to bring in two striking images which they like. They should then explain the links and contrasting elements which they are making between the two images. Ask other students to make further links. To consolidate this skill, ask students to say what they have learned through comparing and contrasting and create a class display to help them in future lessons.

Following a line of logic

"Following an argument really makes us think — is this really true?"

Once students have explored the idea that argument is not necessarily purely emotional — it also involves reasoning and explanation — you can move students towards developing their logical responses.

Make sure students have the vocabulary for logical argument, for example:

should, must, ought, necessarily, since, because, for, as, in as much as, for the reason that, first, therefore, hence, thus, so, consequently, it follows that, from this.

Give students a set of sentences such as the following:

All Year 8 students are going on a trip.
Sam is in Year 8.
Therefore Sam is going on a trip.

Discuss how the conclusion followed from the information given in the first two statements.

Next, ask students to fill in the gaps:

1) We always eat chips on a Friday.
2)
3) We will eat chips tomorrow.

Next, ask students in pairs to set each other these simple, three-line logic puzzles. If any are not logical or cause argument, ask students to note down why. It will often be because one or both of the premises is faulty for one reason or another, for example:

1) Girls are better than boys.
2) Halima is a girl and Jake is a boy.
3) Halima is better than Jake.

This is likely to provoke discussion, so ask students to write down what makes an argument logical and then agree a set of rules.

Familiar and similar?

"I learned loads of new words doing this exercise!"

This task asks students to differentiate clearly between words that are fairly similar in meaning. Not only does this allow for a discussion about how we understand words and how we use them, but it also moves students towards greater precision in their writing.

Give students pairs of words such as:

Confident/big-headed
Learn/know
Assertive/aggressive
Love/adore.

Ask students to discuss in pairs what they think the differences and similarities are between the words and then to come up with their own definitions for each. Students should then listen to each other's definitions and agree on those which they feel most appropriate. Ask students to look up definitions of any words they don't know after they have guessed the meaning.

Next ask them to come up with a range of synonyms for each of the words and ask them to go through them again to tease out the differences and similarities.

Now ask the class to select unfamiliar words from either the class reader or a book they are reading. With a thesaurus they should research alternative words and again tease out the differences. These exercises will really stretch their language development.

Taking it further

Ask students to research the roots or etymology of some of the words they find most interesting. Collate these on a class board for future reference.

Connections, connections

"Making connections between random objects was hard at first, but then I kept seeing new ways of linking things together. It's really made me think."

Helping students to understand connecting ideas is important for properly engaging with a text. Students enjoy making surprising links and when they do so they are building their vocabulary for analysing and explaining key ideas.

Teaching tip

If you are short on time, provide students with a set of words printed individually on cards and choose the categories. Ask students to sort the words into the most appropriate category.

Bonus idea ★

Try this idea in another media! Ask students to choose two pictures or two pieces of music and make the links between them. They could use this to lead a starter and ask the class to come up with other connecting ideas between the two works. This works well using the 'Think, Pair, Share' strategy.

Ask students to give you a word that they associate with a class reader they have just finished, or a short story they have just read. The words do not have to be plot-related at all, but simply the first word that comes to mind when the student thinks of the text (ask them not to use generic positive or negative words such as 'boring' or, 'excellent'). Aim for around 20–30 words. Note these on your board and then ask students, in groups, to decide on four or five categories into which they could place the words. A word can be used in more than one category, but all words must be used. Students can add any words they feel important during the exercise. For example, for Harry Potter, students could choose the categories of 'Magic', 'Friendship', 'Good vs. Evil' and so on.

Students then prepare a presentation explaining their choices of category and their decisions. Ask students to present their findings as a poster, illustrating their key categories and ideas and then discussing them with the class.

Justifying your position

"Deciding which order to put things in means we have to be prepared to give our reasons – and agree to disagree sometimes!"

This exercise encourages thinking, reasoning and justifying. There is no absolute right or wrong position and students may well agree on different hierarchies. This is fine because it is the reasons for the position that are important.

Give students cards printed with information such as key characters or important events from a studied text, school rules, moral standpoints, ingredients for a successful friendship. Ask students to work in small groups to arrange these cards in rank order, justifying and debating about positioning. Students then present their order back to the class. It is useful to encourage dialogue here so as to afford students the chance to explore the ideas of others and justify their own. The class then agrees a whole-class order. This could be organised as a diamond or pyramid rather than a simple ascending line but, of course, the organisational shape you use brings with it its own dilemmas.

Next, give students cards featuring a number of events – these can be text descriptions or images. In small groups, ask students to arrange the events in a sequence that makes sense to them and to justify the order. It may help to display a number of connectives such as 'subsequently', but be sure that students understand the relationship suggested by each connective, and ask them to connect the events using each connective once only. Students tell their version of events to the whole class.

Taking it further

Ask students in groups to select their own text and to identify and take out statements for other students to put in order. Encourage them to justify why they put some elements in a higher ranking or position.

Writing

Part 6

Get a grip on handwriting

"Sometimes in their rush to get ideas down, students' handwriting can suffer. I have a regular session called 'I can see clearly now!' where we look at the quality of their handwriting. Above all, clear handwriting is about being courteous to the reader!"

For many students, word-processing has been a real boon. Not only can they check spelling and grammar — with quite unusual results at times — but also their words can be seen clearly and unambiguously. While this is a real benefit, students still need to be able to write legibly in longhand, both in class and in examinations.

Teaching tip

Ask students to find examples of handwriting, some of which are difficult and others easy to read, and encourage them to talk about the difference between the two. They should link this back to their own handwriting and work out how they could make their own work clearer.

While many individuals will find it almost impossible to develop textbook handwriting — particularly during the hurried environment of the examination room — it is possible to provide students with some tips and exercises which will help them control their writing and make it much easier to decipher. Teaching students 'joined up' writing can help with their spelling, as patterns are learned and remembered.

First, make sure that students are sitting up, with both feet on the floor and leaning forward a little towards the desk. The paper should be in line with the shoulder of their writing hand, rather than in the middle of the desk. Pens should be held by the thumb and forefinger, with the middle finger giving further support, depending on what feels most comfortable.

Ask students to practise their grip and holding the pen by moving the pen up and down the page in diagonal and vertical strokes.

Taking it further

To further develop motor memory, ask students to draw some controlled circles and waves, paying attention to size and consistency. This can be especially important now that students write by hand less and less frequently.

Try to ensure that the pen strokes are as regular as possible and students are controlling their pens rather than just scribbling on the page. This can help students develop a 'motor' memory. Think about how you sometimes need to write a word to check its spelling — that is your motor memory at work.

Refining handwriting skills

"While many students will have learnt how to form letters when they were in their primary school, I have found that they often get into bad habits. If the goal is to make their work as clear to their reader as possible then I tell them I want to see well-crafted letters!"

It is important to focus on clarity rather than notions of 'correctness' because handwriting is very individual.

Many students do not form their letters completely. Focus students' attention on the difference in size and relationship to the line between, for example, 'd', 'a' and 'j'. This needs to be emphasised, particularly as many students (often girls for some reason) write each letter the same height and width, resulting in a difficult-to-read 'fat bubble' effect. You may also want to remind students that the letter 'i' is not topped with circles, stars, flowers or hearts, but with a simple dot.

Ask them to write the alphabet quickly (not joined at this point), ensuring that each letter is properly formed. Letters with 'tails' such as 'g' and 'y' should be roughly twice the size of those without, as should capital letters. For some students, this sort of clarity will be improvement enough, but others could move on to tasks which encourage appropriate joining of letters.

Keeping the alphabet on display, ask students to write a selection of words that are joined in a variety of ways, such as: college, date, spoon, twist, should, jump, teach, week, jam.

Having already checked students' work during the exercise, select individuals to come to the front of the class and share what they have done. Extend the task by giving them further words or a short paragraph to write. The time spent on each element and the degree of guidance provided will depend very much on the needs of the class or student.

Teaching tip

Try giving a handwriting exercise as a lesson starter and praise those whose handwriting improves the most. Use a visualiser (see Idea 18) to show the most improved handwriting and ask students to take photos of samples of handwriting over a few weeks. They will be surprised at the improvement as this is one area where practice really does make a difference.

The power of images

"I want my students to write at length but I found that if I asked them to start writing, their responses were a bit thin. When I found a picture related to the topic I wanted them to write about I found that their responses were longer and better developed. It really was a case of 'a picture telling a thousand words'!"

Pictures can be used to great effect in the classroom as a way of exploring an idea or character; initiating questions; summing up or recapping; exploring connections and emotions – the possibilities are considerable.

Teaching tip

Collect striking and puzzling images and encourage your students to do the same. Websites such as *Guardian* Eye Witness www.theguardian.com/world/series/eyewitness and the BBC News in Pictures www.bbc.co.uk/news/in_pictures provide stimulating material on a daily basis.

Bonus idea ★

Read a short story. The students have to 'retell' it by selecting 4–5 pictures. This is a useful way of seeing what points of the story they feel are most important and also how they interpret the story. It can lead to quite varied responses, which can in turn lead to interesting discussions.

As English teachers, we often spend the bulk of our time focused firmly on the written word. While this is both necessary and understandable, pictures also have an important role to play in the English classroom. Most examination boards use pictures in some form, for example, where students analyse or comment upon images used in non-fiction texts such as advertisements or newspapers. Others may use an image to kick-start a piece of descriptive writing. By using images in our classrooms, we can help students to succeed in exams and reach those who find text difficult to access. It also gives students the opportunity to explore meaning on their own terms and in their own way.

Show some interesting images to the students and allow them to look at the images for a few moments in silence, before writing their responses on Post-its and then sharing them with their neighbour. The students' ideas can be fed back to the whole class, and a selection can be noted on the board. Ask the students to write a sentence or short paragraph about the images using their own and others' suggestions. This takes the stress out of writing immediately at length and extends their repertoire of vocabulary and imagery.

Using images

"Images are high challenge, low threat! What I was looking for was a way of getting students talking in more depth about characters. I have found that images get students talking in detail about the characters in a novel or play."

Images can stimulate ideas and create space for analogies and speculation. They encourage students to talk about their ideas before writing them down.

Set out a selection of pictures and ask students to choose the one they feel most represents a character from the text you are working on in class, or an aspect of that character, and to explain their choice. For example, one of my students chose a picture of a derelict block of flats to represent Macbeth as he felt that the flats once had great promise, but were now just a bad reminder of what could have been.

Similarly, students select a picture they feel best represents how a character may be feeling at a given time. Again, encourage your students to explain their choices. It is through their explanations that they begin to explore meaning and often, unencumbered by text, many students find they are able to explain their choices in quite sophisticated ways.

These pictures can also be used as stimulus for discussion and debate, or students could select or bring in pictures of their own that they think sum up a particular point of view, for example, an animal in a cage perhaps, or a landfill site. These can then be explored as a whole class with teacher guidance.

Teaching tip

Ask students to select an image they find striking or about which they want to learn more. In groups of three, they must choose the picture that raises the most interesting questions. Try to guide students away from questions *about* the image as such and towards questions *raised* by the image. For example, a picture of an empty room may begin a discussion on loneliness – carefully facilitated by you. This approach owes a lot to Philosophy for Children – something that can play a very important role in our classrooms.

Structuring stories

"I love stories and I want my students to love them too! However, when they come to write their own, they need to know how to structure them. One of the best ways of doing this is to get them to work out what the key features of a great story are."

Writing a good story is not necessarily an innate gift and some of the basic mechanics can be taught to improve the story-writing skills of all students.

Teaching tip

Professional writers in film and advertising create 'storyboards' to show the flow of the narrative, the broader scenes and background notes to characters and plot. These help the writers and film makers to visualise the story and are a good way of spotting anything that might be missing. Ask students to create their own storyboards and to use a sample to be shown through the visualiser to check against the basic planning format.

It is sometimes thought that the 'story' is the form of writing most easily accessible to students. After all, they have been writing them for most of their school lives and are familiar with the form. The activities in this idea can be used to focus students on features of a good story and encourage them to improve their own writing. Some of the suggestions below may help to focus students on writing effective and engaging stories.

- Divide the class into groups and distribute three (very) short stories to each. Ask students to put the stories in rank order and to write a brief explanation for their decision.
- Introduce students to the basic planning format of: opening; plot/character development; problem; conclusion/ resolution.
- Read through one of the extracts with them, indicating how the story would fit this format. Students then write the plan for their favourite of the three extracts, using this format. You can use students' knowledge of films or urban myths to reinforce this planning format.
- Give students a genre, such as the spooky story, and ask them to write a plan for their own story using the format.

- Next, distribute the opening paragraphs from three stories, each of which should be effective in a different way. Ask students to identify – individually or in pairs – key features such as: narrative voice used; any words or phrases that hint at what is to come; a detailed description of a place, person or object; opening sentence; any characters or situations that are introduced; what action occurs. If possible, students comment on what effect any of these features helps create. Students feed back to the class and share ideas. From the feedback, produce a list of effective elements.
- Get students to play around with the story openings you have selected. They can change the mood, the intended audience, the tense, or the type of imagery used. It is useful for students to practise engaging actively with text in this way. You can later get them to explore it as, say, a letter, diary entry or newspaper article to show them how text type and conventions impact upon content.

Shared writing can be used effectively here, particularly for those students who need to focus on improving their narrative writing skills. As a class, construct an effective opening paragraph for a story. You can alter vocabulary, structure, imagery and so on through (guided) consensus. Remember to demonstrate the writing process for your students. Talk the process through, deciding which word is more effective than another, whether one image works or if it could be improved. Remember to focus on developing them as writers. Get them to write!

Taking it further

Ask students to choose which opening they find most effective and use this to model the opening to their own story. If time allows, volunteers read their story openings and students raise their hand each time a particular effect is noticed and explain what they have spotted.

Establishing character

"The real difference in bringing stories to life is helping students to get under the skin of their characters. I realised that students were able to do this whenever we talked about a character in one of the soap operas and that they could use these skills to do the same when developing the characters in their writing."

Helping students to recognise how characters are created is one of the most important ways we can develop their analysis skills and also develop their own craft of writing.

Teaching tip

Ask students to find character descriptions either from a class text or something they are reading for pleasure. Ask them to research one character type in depth to create a class bank of characters to share.

Taking it further

Ask students to take one of the characters created by someone else from the class and to write up their own version. Ask them to say what was particularly helpful and what could be improved. You could also ask them to swap characters and construct a scenario – based on their understanding of each character- where these characters first meet.

Read through three descriptions of characters with the class. Ask the class to note how we learn about each character. From their observations draw a class mind map on the board, including points such as: how a character looks, what they say and how they speak, how other characters react to them, any imagery used to describe them and so on.

Distribute to pairs of students cards that identify two characters, their relationship, basic characteristics and, most importantly, how you want readers to react towards the characters. Each pair then writes a paragraph together that sets the characters up for the reader. Select paragraphs to be read aloud and ask students to note down how they feel about the characters, and why they feel that way. After the reading, students share their observations.

Creating atmosphere

"When our teacher got us really thinking about what happens when we react to something scary and helped us to use different ways of getting this across to our reader, I understood what she meant when she said 'Let's get more power into our prose!'"

Students need to inject detail and atmosphere into their stories.

Draw an outline 'map' of a body on the board. Ask students to do the same in their books, leaving plenty of room around their drawing for labelling. Start a discussion about how the body reacts when people are scared, for example, hair stands on end, shivers run up the spine and so on. Label the body on the board with one example and explain that they have 5–10 minutes to label their drawings with as many reactions as they can. While students are engaged in this, it is useful to monitor their responses and pick up on any particularly interesting examples you may wish to call on later – as well as those you may want to avoid!

Once their time is up, invite students up to the board to label the drawing with one of their examples. When you feel the labelling on the board is detailed enough, ask students to copy down any suggestions they may have missed, so that each student has a complete set of reactions labelled on their drawing. This can also be captured through a visualiser or photograph and used as a prompt for other writing exercises. This can, of course, be adapted to fit other emotions, such as love. Students then write five short sentences featuring their observations.

Teaching tip

This sort of task can help students write more effectively. Model an example for them so that they can see the impact it can have. Getting into the habit of writing ' My heart started beating faster and the hairs on the back of my neck stood up' instead of 'I was scared' will make students writing have more impact on the reader and marker!

Bonus idea ★

Move from this to a piece of shared writing with the class where their ideas are used as the basis for a piece of descriptive writing.

Creating a sense of place

"If we really want to power up our students' writing we need to make sure they pay attention to thinking about and describing the key features and atmosphere of a place."

Creating a great description that captures the sense of place is something students need to understand in order to progress in their writing. Students are often good at describing characters but they need help to do the same with places.

This is a follow-up activity to the 'map of the body' in idea 47. It can be adapted to fit many types of story or can be used as a stand-alone task. The focus here is on the setting. Draw the outline of a house on the board and ask the students to copy it into their books. Ask students to think about elements that could create a scary atmosphere there. Discussion may be initiated by asking students to think about what scares them when they are alone in a house. Label the drawing with one example, such as creaking floorboards, or the eyes of a painting that seem to follow you. Again, give students between 5–10 minutes to label their own drawings and then feed back to the class. Once sufficient ideas have been collected, students copy any suggestions they might have missed.

Then bring in the 'map of the body' by asking students to write five compound or complex sentences using the information found in their drawings. Write down two features from the drawing of the body and two from that of the house, then ask students to connect them to make two sentences, such as:

As the door creaked open a shiver ran down my spine.

Teaching tip

Be sure to use students' knowledge from other lessons to inform their writing. Effective dialogue; variety in sentence structure; thoughtful selection of verbs, adverbs and adjectives; narrative voice and use of alliteration, metaphor and simile can all help to make writing about place more effective.

Bonus idea ★

Another great way to help students achieve a sense of place in their writing is to get them to think about places as characters.

Sizzling similes

"Now let's turn to simile, close cousin to the metaphor."

Teaching students the difference between metaphor and simile is important and also quite simple. Metaphors make direct connections while similes use links such as 'like' or 'as' to signal to the reader that there is a link between the two ideas.

Gather a range of similes such as:

cute as a kitten

as busy as a bee

as snug as a bug in a rug

as black as coal

as blind as a bat.

Ask students to give their ideas on the bigger impressions being created by each simile. Show students a range of images from websites such as *Guardian* Eye Witness and ask them to make connections with everyday items. Then ask them to come up with their own examples.

Take examples of some of creative writing and show them to the class using a visualiser. Ask the students to come up with ideas for how some well-chosen similes would make the piece richer, more interesting and a better read. Then do the same with some examples of students' work. Remind them that their suggestions should be relevant and kind.

Taking it further

Ask students to create their own versions of the key differences between simile and metaphor. Get them to include some of their favourite examples, compare notes and stake a claim for theirs being the best!

Identifying metaphor and simile

"Students use metaphor and simile quite frequently, although they may not recognise it as such. I wanted to find a way to make the implicit explicit!"

Phrases such as 'I am boiling', 'stop acting like a baby', 'she's cool' and so on are regular features of the soundscape of a school. While students may use metaphor and simile readily in their everyday speech, they need to understand how they are identified and how they work. They then need to know how to use this understanding effectively in their own reading and writing.

Teaching tip

Ask students to research the etymology of 'simile' and 'metaphor'. Knowing that metaphor comes from the Greek for 'carrying over' will help them to understand that using one idea to give new information about a second idea is very powerful. In the same way, the Latin root for simile will help them to understand how comparisons work. Remember too, that in and of itself a simile or a metaphor does not make better writing. Be sure to stress the impact as well as the structure.

Give students a definition for both metaphor and simile, emphasising that metaphor describes one thing *as if it is another* and simile uses the words *as* or *like*. These things needn't be laboured – the effect is, after all, more important. A secure grounding in definition is useful, however. Next, distribute examples of metaphors and similes written on individual cards. Ask students to divide them into either metaphors or similes. The class share responses and any anomalies or difficulties are discussed.

Select a few common examples of metaphors and similes and display them to the class. Ask the class to write down what each suggests, as well as the literal meaning such as:

'It's cool' means something is OK (metaphor).

'It's cool' means something is a cold (literal).

Literal and figurative

"Helping students realise the power of metaphor and simile is essential. But they also need to find ways of knowing when something is literal as opposed to figurative. I found that students enjoy doing this sort of analysis."

The class need to understand that figurative (metaphorical) use is very different from literal. Metaphors and similes generally compare two things that are different in most ways except for one.

Direct students' attention back to the examples of similes and metaphors introduced in ideas 49 and 50 and ask them to write alongside each example what element is being identified as similar. For example: 'You pig' compares the way someone eats to that of a pig. Ask students to select the most likely comparison from examples such as the following:

That test was rock hard:

a) It was made of a solid substance, like rock.
b) It was difficult to get through.

My love is like the sun:

a) She is big, round and yellow.
b) She is the centre of everything for me.

The main aim is to encourage students to think about what is being suggested by a metaphor or a simile. They can also use this format to write about metaphor and simile. For example:

The simile 'my love is like the sun' suggests that she is the centre of the writer's universe.

Display some sentence starters and ask students to complete them using metaphor or simile. For example:

Peter sprinted down the pitch like . . .
Her skin felt like . . .

Teaching tip

Again, impact is key here. Often student learn the mechanics of using metaphor without really understanding the intended impact. Explore *why* 'Sam was a pig' has more impact than 'Sam is messy when he eats'.

Bonus idea ★

Guide students towards metaphors that do not use 'is' as a marker, such as:

My mind raced through the possible answers.

He appeared, an angry bull ready to knock down anything in his way.

Students underline any words that are used metaphorically and describe what effect the metaphor has.

Formal and informal language

"The ability to know the difference between formal and informal language is one of the most important ways of helping students to refine their writing. They need to be reminded that this is what sets out the best quality responses in exams!"

One of the easiest ways to introduce the idea of informal and formal language is to teach students how to structure a formal letter.

Teaching tip

Be sure to emphasise the importance of audience and purpose here. Structure, language choice and tone are drawn from there. Pragmatics is the key!

Taking it further

Ask students to write an informal and a formal letter or email about the same topic, but to different audiences. For example, a letter to your sister/the police complaining about a noisy neighbour; a postcard to a friend/boss.

Bonus idea ★

Ask students to produce a talk for a given pair of audiences about the same topic. This is also a good time to remind them of the information that body language can provide and tone of voice. This can be done as a starter or way in to exploring formal and informal register.

Prepare a model pair of letters – one formal, the other informal – that are on the same basic subject. Distribute copies to the class or present them on the IWB. Ask students to write down the audience and purpose of each letter. For example, Letter A is for a friend and describes a holiday, and Letter B is for a customer and is selling a holiday. In a table, students then write down the main features from each letter that helped them decide who the audience was and the purpose of the letter. This can include features such as layout, greeting, vocabulary and so on. For example, were paragraphs used differently, did the letters address the recipient differently and were they signed off differently?

Use this task to produce a short and clear set of criteria for formal and informal letters, which are recorded in students' books. Distribute to each student a slip of paper with an audience, for example, 'grandparent', and purpose, for example, 'Thanking them for the jumper they gave you (again) for your birthday'; or 'Local newspaper' and 'Complaining about the mess in a local park'. Students then write a short letter using this and the rules as their guideline.

You can also give them examples that have inappropriate elements, for example, a letter for a job that uses slang or has kisses at the end, and ask them to identify which parts they would keep and which need to be changed.

Writing to describe

"This type of writing is often more difficult than it seems. Students tend towards writing narrative rather than description and so this needs special focus."

The aim here is to make students' writing as vivid and original as possible. When they get the hang of this, the quality of their writing improves significantly and their enjoyment in working up great descriptions also increases.

Ask students to imagine they are in a familiar environment, such as the school canteen, and to think of what they see, hear, smell, taste and touch. Reinforce the idea of paying close attention to everything they can think of – getting them to close their eyes can be useful here. For example, rather than the door being simply white, is it freshly painted? Graffiti-covered? Most of the description offered will be of things seen or heard, but emphasise the need to create as complete a picture as possible using the other senses too, where appropriate. Complete a class mind map with all their observations. Students then write each of the observations under the appropriate sense in their books.

Next show students a film you have made of this place, pausing at key points to read some of their descriptions or to focus on any aspects that were missed out. Include sound as well as image here.

Next, ask students to write a short description of a familiar place or thing using as many of the senses as they can, but without naming what it is they are describing. Volunteers read their work to the class who have to guess what is being described.

Taking it further

Ask students to write about the best place they have ever been in. Students swap descriptions and draw one another's places based on the description given. The drawing is then returned to the student whose room it is, to see if it is accurate. Any discrepancies can be discussed.

Writing to persuade

"When our students become competent at recognising and using persuasive language, not only will their writing improve, they will become better at helping others to understand their point of view."

Students are familiar with the types of persuasive text and the language used in this idea. Advertisements bombard them from every angle and many students are themselves quite skilled in the art of persuasion!

Many students find it surprisingly difficult to work out explicitly *how* these types of text work. It is therefore often best to pick a few specific and familiar features of persuasive text and focus on these rather than risk muddying the waters with an exhaustive list of examples.

Distribute, in whichever way suits you and your class best, a glossary of persuasive devices such as: the rhetorical question; rule of three; 'stick and carrot'; hyperbole; repetition; use of emotive language; flattery; etc. In pairs, ask students to role-play the following scenario.

A teenager is desperate to go to a birthday party at a friend's house. Their parent is adamant that, following the teenager's late arrival home after the last party, they will not be allowed to go. The teenager's task is to persuade the parent to change their mind, using as many techniques as they can.

Many students may find it difficult to sustain an argument for very long. Ensure that students are familiar with devices so that they can be used to frame their attempts at persuasion. Monitor the exercise and select good examples to show to the rest of the class, asking the class to tick off any persuasive techniques they spot.

Telling my story

"Writing about my life and hearing what others had written about theirs was very moving. I actually learnt a lot about myself that I hadn't realised until I wrote it down."

Just like everyone else, students like talking about themselves – the interesting things in their lives, the things that matter to them and what they think about life. Before they do this in writing they need time to think about and organise their ideas.

Autobiographical writing has several positive elements, perhaps the most important of which is giving students the opportunity to write about an area in which they are the expert. It can be accessed by students of different abilities and can draw on a variety of skills.

Give the class extracts from well-known autobiographical works to read through. Ask the class to identify key features of autobiographical writing: use of the first person; exploration of thoughts and feelings; one-sided perspective; selection and editing etc. From these extracts create a set of guidelines to display throughout the series of lessons.

Remind students that autobiographical works do not tell every detail of a life but rather select key elements. Self-editing is an important skill here. Ask the class to think of a memorable story from their time at junior school. They should consider why this is an important memory for them. Is it humorous, sad, tense? Did it change them? Did they learn something from it? Did it change others' opinions of them? Students then share their stories in pairs. You can repeat the activity with memorable holidays, parties or school trips. There may be a degree of sensitivity required in some instances as students' circumstances and experiences may vary greatly.

Teaching tip

Share the key aspects of the autobiographies on a visualiser. Ask students to suggest what made the extracts from the autobiography compelling and add these. Tell the students that identifying the most compelling aspects of the writing will help them to write their own.

Writing my story

"Write about something that happened to you when . . ."

When students have had the chance to identify what makes powerful impressions in other people's autobiographies, they should be sufficiently stimulated to want to write their own.

Plan some activities to give students starting points and inspiration for writing their own autobiographies and to help them break it up into manageable chunks:

- Complete a timeline of your life so far, indicating one key memory (or more) for each year.
- Keep an image diary of key places and people, for example, sketches of your old school, friends or family members; photos; detailed descriptions of bedrooms or favourite toys.
- Bring in an object that holds strong memories (be sure that parents are informed), for example, a favourite toy, a gift from a grandparent, a holiday memento. Explain to the class the reasons why that object is so important.
- Create a coat of arms for yourself using those things they feel represent them.

Students can then develop these ideas and write pieces based on the different topics, for example, my earliest memory, first day at school, memories of junior school, my family, proudest day, my future. If possible and appropriate, encourage students to research their family stories.

More ideas to develop autobiographical writing

"The sky's the limit when it comes to stimulating students' ideas and language. Using sounds, sights and smells will open up their readiness to describe their own experiences."

There are many rewarding tasks and ideas that can be used when students are writing autobiographical pieces; not only because students can explore a variety of text types and utilise a range of skills but also because it allows the class to find out more about each other, encouraging students to reflect and consider those events, people and things that are most significant to them and why.

Ask students to bring in a copy of their first favourite song or songs that remind them of specific events such as their first school disco, a holiday or Christmas. Music can be incredibly evocative and students often find that their memories are awoken by one another's choices. Similarly, smell is very evocative. In sealed jars, bring in smells such as some fresh grass, baby powder, vinegar, pine needles or bubble bath. Ask blindfolded students to smell a selected jar and then to describe to the class any memories that the smell may evoke.

Students interview one another using prepared questions. These are then presented either in written form as a magazine Q&A, for example, or as a television/radio interview. Alternatively, students could produce a print, radio or television advert for their autobiographies, selecting those elements they think will attract a readership and presenting them accordingly.

Taking it further

Get students to use their drama skills to present aspects of their life stories, for example, tableaus and thought tracking can be very effective. Ask students to script key scenes from their lives and perform them in groups – the author acting as director. See idea 85 for more details.

Let's write together!

"Writing together helps me see there is more than one way to go about something."

Working through ideas with others generates bigger and better ideas. Students who might be insecure as writers can really benefit from this sort of collaborative modelling and those who are more confident get an opportunity to think explicitly about what they may do intuitively.

Teaching tip

During the shared collaborative element of the lesson, model the writing thought process for the students. This is especially important in the early stages of using this sort of approach. Talk about why one word may be more effective, or why one part should be moved. This approach can be used equally effectively for non-fiction texts.

Organise the students into groups of four or five. Agree as a class the kind of story you will write, for example a travel story or science fiction, and then set each group the task of creating a character for the story. Each group then feeds back, outlining their character and explaining why they would be good for the story. The class then agree, with your guidance, on which characters they are going to use. The class then work on the opening of their story.

Ask students to work in small groups to come up with sentences which are then shared with the class. These are then modified by the class, for example, adjectives can be added, punctuation altered, or actions dropped in or removed. Be sure to direct focus onto the impact that certain words or phrases have. This shared modelling can best be done using an IWB or flipchart .It is important that students can see the editing and drafting process as it occurs. Aim to get as many different contributions as you can. The collaborative group nature of the writing needs to be reinforced and the decisions made about the shared text should come from the whole class as far as possible.

Alternatively, write an opening collaborative paragraph as a class and then ask students to complete the rest of the story individually or in their groups, using what they have learned from the collaborative exercise.

Reading body language

"Look for non-verbal clues!"

We all recognise signs that let us know how someone is feeling before they have spoken a word. A closer examination of body language and what meaning we can read from it can be of great benefit to students as readers and writers of text.

Ask the class to stand up and shake their limbs gently. When they hear you shout an emotion, they are to freeze in a pose that depicts that emotion. Call students' attention to any particularly good representations. Extend this by giving individual students specific emotions to pose for the class.

Then, put students into pairs and give them a series of three or four emotions. These are to be acted out without noise as part of a sequence. Selected pairs show their sequence to the class who guess the emotions being illustrated.

Next, give students a text extract that has spaces for body language to be added. Above each space, write the emotion that is to be presented through clues given by the body. For example, these might be surprise, sadness or doubt. Students complete the passage, selecting appropriate body language. The passage is then read through with volunteers filling the gaps with their selections. Students then compile a dictionary of the body, giving examples of body language and possible meanings. Students use the results of this exercise to revisit an earlier piece of writing to make it more interesting and complex.

Taking it further

Ask students to research what psychologists say about body language. They then create brief summaries and compare notes to extend their ideas for writing about body language.

Fiction

Part 7

Get under their skin

"What I love about English is that we have to think hard about what makes someone tick. It's great trying understand what someone is really like."

A thorough understanding of character is the key into narrative texts for many students. It is also a good way to begin teaching close analysis of text, lending itself as it does to close reading and inference. We can find out about a character in many ways, for example, what they do and how, the way they look, what they say and how others react to them.

Teaching tip

Encourage students to use deduction to gather information and gain deeper insight into character. Reinforce that writers create characters and make careful decisions about how they look, what they say and so on to create a particular impression. Dickens is, of course, very useful for this sort of thing.

These exercises encourage students to explore why they react to certain characters in particular ways.

Students read the following passages and then answer the questions underneath.

Steven shuffled into the classroom, his gaze fixed firmly on his grubby, unfashionable trainers. He had always been small for his age – quiet, too. He hadn't just 'grown up and out of it' as his mum had promised him so many times.

'Maybe if I stay just here, they won't notice me,' he thought to himself.

There was to be no such luck.

'Nice shoes, Mouseboy! Look at them. What a state!'

The whole class turned to look, their laughter turning his face an even deeper shade of red.

- How do you think Steven feels about entering his classroom? Which word or words make you think that? What does this tell you about him?
- Do you think he has felt this way for a while? What makes you think that? What could this tell us about Steven?

- What do you think his classmates think of him? Why do you think that? What might this tell us about Steven?

Use these questions in a class discussion about the text. Use sentence starters to help students refer to the text, for example: 'Steven is . . .' 'I think this because in the passage it says . . .'

Now do the same using this description of Harry Potter from J.K. Rowling's *Harry Potter and the Philosopher's Stone*:

Harry had always been small and skinny for his age . . . Harry had a thin face, knobbly knees, black hair and bright green eyes. He wore round glasses held together with a lot of cellotape because of all the times Dudley had punched him in the nose. The only thing Harry liked about his appearance was a very thin scar on his forehead which was shaped like a bolt of lightning.

And this description of Calpurnia in Harper Lee's *To Kill a Mockingbird*

She was all angles and bones; she was nearsighted; she squinted; her hand was wide as a bed slat and twice as hard. She was always ordering me out of the kitchen, asking me why I couldn't behave as well as Jem when she knew he was older, and calling me home when I wasn't ready to come. Our battles were epic and one-sided. Calpurnia always won, mainly because Atticus always took her side. She had been with us ever since Jem was born, and I had felt her tyrannical presence as long as I could remember.

Atomising atmosphere!

"I found that creating atmosphere helps students add power and depth to their writing."

The same basic skills developed in creating character can be used to understand atmosphere. Through close reading, students are encouraged to identify *how* a particular impression is created.

These tasks and skills help students develop their writing skills by showing students explicitly how writers create certain effects – skills that they can then employ in their own writing. The following tasks help students build awareness of how certain effects are created. Ask students to read the following sentence carefully:

Sara skipped through the sun-dappled woods. Birds sang sweetly from the lush, green trees and the ground felt soft beneath her feet.

The picture created here is very sweet and pleasant, almost like a Disney film.

Next, get students to consider how just a few word replacements can change atmosphere:

Sara crept through the storm-struck woods. Birds screeched menacingly from the bare, overgrown trees and the ground felt brittle beneath her feet.

Just by changing a few words, a totally different atmosphere is created.

Ask students to transform the following sentence so that the atmosphere changes from calm to chaotic:

The school canteen was full of well-behaved children chatting quietly and the sweet smell of delicious food.

See if they can identify what kind of words are changed. Nouns? Adjectives? Verbs? Adverbs?

Let's read together!

"Having the whole class read a text is a great way of sharing literature, sharing responses and modelling high quality writing."

There is great benefit in asking students to recall the themes, characters, settings or plot points from something they read when they were younger. They can then use these ideas and apply them to a new class text.

Before starting a new whole class novel, get students to use the information provided by its cover to predict what the book will be about. Ask students to note down their thoughts on what type of story they think it will be, where and when it is set, who the main characters will be and any ideas about plot they may have. If any particular themes are identified, ask the class for their opinions. This sort of prediction task is a useful way of introducing key ideas and it also encourages students to develop their skills of deduction. As students take any piece of work more seriously if they know that it has an audience, say to them, 'We are about to read a book together as a class. We will be talking about and writing about what we like and don't like about it. Who else might be interested in what we think about the novel?' This could be students in other classes, family or friends. Identifying the audience for their comments will help them to further analyse and learn from the novel.

Set up a class blog to capture work in progress and to provide a finished product for a wider audience to read. Students could research websites which specialise in reviews of books such as www.goodreads.com and come up with their own version which could be published on the school website.

Taking it further

It can be very powerful to choose a text that relates to other subject areas. For example, students could read *All Quiet on the Western Front* (Erich Maria Remarque) if they are studying the First World War in history, or they could use *Silent Spring* (Rachel Carson) as a companion piece to geography or science lessons. This encourages discussion across departments and helps students make links between subjects.

Character building

"I'm stuck on describing a character!"

Encouraging students to empathise with a character brings characters to life, makes them vivid, realistic and ready to leap off the page. These activities help students to understand and relate to the characters they are studying by imagining what they look like, getting them to step into their skin and think from their point of view.

The following activities will help students to develop their characters:

- Read a detailed character description as a class, ask students to draw the character, using the description as their guide. This is not about their art skills, but about helping them to see that good physical descriptions can be translated into images. Students then write a few sentences exploring how the description made them feel about the character, giving reasons for their opinions.
- Students create character fact files that contain a drawing and key information, such as age, family and interests. These can be used in later tasks, for example, writing a profile on a class blog.
- Use 'hot seating' as a way of exploring character. Allocate characters to students and ask them to prepare to answer questions about a particular incident or theme. This can be organised in a chat-show format with several characters appearing as guests, which will encourage students to think about relationships in the novel.
- If a particular problem presents itself in the narrative, students write a letter in character to an agony aunt as well as a reply offering advice. Remind students to write *as* the character, voicing the *character's* concerns in *their* voice. To reinforce this skill, ask students to write a diary or a letter to a friend.

Empathy tasks are a good way for students to show that they have really got to grips with a character. In order to gain the best mark they are capable of, students need to show not only an understanding of the part a character plays in a narrative, but also that they can express thoughts and feelings that character may have and (for the top levels) use the voice of that character convincingly.

For all empathy tasks it is vital that students understand that they are writing *as* a given character rather than *about* them. This necessitates them writing from that character's point of view rather than simply retelling the story in the first person. Ask students to write down key things that must be remembered when writing in character. These should include: using the first person throughout; offering the character's viewpoint on events found in the text and accurate references to setting, period and relationships.

Taking it further

Focus in specifically on the language a given character may use. This can help students develop a sense of character's voice and help them when responding to texts as well as in their own writing.

Bonus idea

You can ask students to critique one another's work through a silent debate. This means that they read one another's ideas carefully and write down their responses or suggestions for taking it further. This is a great way of concentrating the mind.

Character profiling

"Building a profile of a character helps students to look closely at what an individual says and does. This increases their enjoyment and builds their ability to make insightful comments about motives."

When students build up detailed knowledge of the attributes of different characters they also build vocabulary, learn to infer and learn how to give reasons for the aspects they have identified. It helps if this is done systematically.

Ask students to write down a 'fact file' containing at least five key facts about a character in a text you are studying, including, for example, name, age, marital status and occupation. Next, ask them to link the character to at least three other characters in the studied text by the nature of their relationship and any important information. For example, in 'Romeo and Juliet' students could use the following structure:

CHARACTER: Nurse

LINK: Care giver to Juliet

The nurse is loyal, loving and secretive. She has nursed Juliet since she was a baby. She only wants what is best for Juliet, even though this means she is prepared to go behind her employer's back.

This stage can be differentiated by asking students to add detail about the type of language, imagery or other features used by the character. For example:

Nurse: She is often distracted and will start one story only to go into another. Her lines are 'bitty', with lots of personal anecdote and lots of punctuation such as exclamation marks and dashes. She sometimes uses inappropriate language.

The amount of detail added at this stage will depend on the students involved and how much guidance and support you think they will need.

Pick a specific focus and ask students to make a spider diagram outlining how the character may feel at this point. In 'Romeo and Juliet', if the focus was, for example, the point where Romeo is banished and Capulet has ordered Juliet to marry Paris, the diagram could include the following information:

NURSE'S FEELINGS:

- Protective of Juliet in the face of her father's anger.
- Upset for Juliet as she knows how much she loves Romeo.
- Worried in case Capulet finds out that she helped them get together.
- Angry and sad about the death of Tybalt.
- Concerned that Juliet makes the 'right' decision and forgets Romeo.

The next stage is to decide what format the piece is to take. It could be a personal letter, an interview, a statement to police, a chapter from an autobiography or a diary entry. What is important is that the students are clear what type of text they are writing and are already familiar with the format. Ask students to write five lines, in character, about one of the points they made in their spider diagram. Check work and ask some students to feed back to the rest of the class.

Taking it further

Focus on language features by showing students a typical piece of dialogue from a character and highlighting the most obvious idiosyncrasies or patterns. Ask students to write a simple instruction or statement in the style of the character using the same images, tone and patterns. Students then share their work. Once you feel all students are clear as to the nature of the task, ask them to complete their piece of writing.

A story within a story

"Chapters provide structure to texts. They help frame a story and students need to know how they help to move a story forward."

Students must be able to recognise the architecture of a novel. Helping them to identify and describe the key elements of a chapter will increase their enjoyment and improve the quality of their analysis.

Teaching tip

At the end of the chapter students write a short prediction for the following chapter. They should use the knowledge available so far in the novel as the basis for their prediction. Ask volunteers to read out their prediction and get them also to state the reasons behind their decision. A discussion can then follow, with other students giving their opinion about the next chapter.

Take the first chapter of a novel as your focus and look at how genre is established through setting, description, language and character. If no obvious genre is established, look at what atmosphere is suggested by time of day, presentation of characters, description of place and use of dialogue.

Give students a photocopied extract of text and explore, for example, what atmosphere is created in the piece. Ask students to read the extract and to underline any features that help create that atmosphere. Then read the extract aloud and instruct students to put up their hands and say 'atmosphere' when any element they have noted is read out. Students have to explain their choice, and, if the class agrees, the point is underlined by all.

This is repeated by considering character, place and use of dialogue. Once all features have been identified, the various sections can be cut out and used as the basis for a reading and understanding written task.

Non-Fiction

Part 8

Text types

"It is so important that students get to grips with the different features of texts. They are going to need this for their exams and when they leave school."

Students will have come across a variety of text types and will know that they are different and have different roles. Talking about the key features of different text types will make their own writing more efficient.

Use the grid below either as an introductory task or as a revision task. It can be used and adapted for any number of text types. Leave a variety of spaces blank, depending on where the grid is to be placed in a sequence of lessons, and ask the class to fill them in.

Text type	Purpose	Layout	Style
Formal letter	To inform, persuade, explain	Date and address Introduction Content Paragraphs Signing off	Dear Sir/Madam Yours faithfully Dear Mr/s Yours sincerely Standard English and a variety of sentence types used
Brochure/leaflet	To persuade, inform	Heading/slogan Illustration Bullet points or short chunks of text Contact information	Use of exaggerated or emotive language and personal pronouns
Advertisement	To persuade	Slogan Illustration Logo	Persuasive language used Personal pronouns often used

Getting to grips with persuasive texts

"It is so important that I teach my students that powerful language can change people's minds."

Students need to have the tools to recognise persuasive techniques in writing and to be confident in using them themselves. They will enjoy seeing the difference it makes to their writing.

Distribute a piece of persuasive writing and, if possible, display a copy on an IWB. There are good examples from sport for example here: www.bbc.co.uk/sport/0/tennis/26540923 or a range of examples here: www.pdst.ie/node/588. Read through the pieces and ask students, in pairs or individually, to identify persuasive techniques, for example, stating the case, giving compelling reasons, issuing a challenge or an invitation to agree. As a class, annotate the piece, encouraging students to note on their own copies any features they may have missed. Using this text as a model, students then produce their own persuasive piece of writing on a topic, the more controversial the better.

Add other tasks to this basic framework: highlight individual features by sentence starters for 'rule of three' or 'stick and carrot' for students to complete; provide vocabulary and phrase banks as a writing frame; extend the introduction to persuasive writing by looking at a variety of persuasive texts, or use the glossary as a task focus, asking students to provide an example for each feature.

Teaching tip

Make sure that students know that persuasive writing will be essential in the world of work. They will need to be able to persuade others in meetings, make their case with clients and ask their boss for a raise! They also need to recognise when texts are written with the aim of persuading them. An informed reader is more equipt to make informed decisions.

Taking it further

Examples of persuasion in films can be found here: www.wingclips.com/themes/persuasion. Ask students to choose one to watch in their own time and report back to the class what makes its message so powerful.

In the news

"I've noticed that students really appreciate having a range of newsprint to look at and compare because they enjoy reading the stories and seeing how differently they have been written up."

While visual image still plays a significant role in the effect created by a newspaper article, the emphasis is much more on the effects created by features of language.

Distribute three versions of the same story – one version written as a front-page newspaper story, while the others may be prose, a diary entry, a letter or any other type of text. Ask students to identify which one is the newspaper story, writing five reasons for their decision on their copy of the story. These will include elements of layout, for example, headline, columns and image.

Next, distribute three texts which have the *layout* of a newspaper front page, only one of which is written in the *style* of a newspaper. Read each piece of text to the class and ask them to again identify which they think is the newspaper story.

Display a class copy of the actual news story through a visualiser and use this to record a guided annotation. Distribute a simple glossary of terms and features to the class. Ask students to identify five features from the list found on the front page. Students then feed back to class and observations should be noted on the class copy. Features to identify include: features of headline such as alliteration, pun or rhyme; any use of the passive voice or tentative language; absence of first-person pronouns except in direct quotation; opening lines outlining story; sequencing (shifting between past, present and future rather than following chronologically); adjective use; identifying people by name, age, appearance, job.

Are all newspapers the same?

"Until I did this exercise, I didn't realise that there were different ways of writing about a news story. I found this really interesting."

Explain to students that the terms 'tabloid' and 'broadsheet' refer to the size of the newspapers. Tabloids are smaller and usually have five columns while broadsheets are larger and have six columns. Most tabloids, such as the *The Sun* are informal in their style of writing and broadsheets such as the *Guardian* have a more formal style.

Distribute a copy of a tabloid front-page story to the class. Display a list of terms, such as headline, caption, byline, columns and so on. First, ask students to identify these terms and label the display copy of front page using students' responses. Next, distribute a broadsheet front page – covering the same story if at all possible. Again label the front page using students' responses.

Ask students to consider the type of vocabulary used, tone, adjective use, sentence length and types of headline. These can be recorded as comprehension answers or in a table.

Give students a selection of events and ask then to write front-page articles about the same story for both a tabloid and a broadsheet newspaper.

Ask the students to compare the two styles of newspapers using the following headings:

- Number of stories on front page
- Size of headline
- Number of words in headline
- Size of image
- Proportion of page covered in text.

Taking it further

Ask students to compare the prices of the different newspapers and circulation figures. Which are more popular? Which might be more profitable? Do they agree that the tabloids tend to have more emotional stories and the broadsheets more factual and political stories? Can they find examples which show the opposite, such as human interest stories in the broadsheets and political analysis in the tabloids?

Sell it to me!

"Oh, those ads are so clever!"

Students need to understand how advertisements work in terms of language, layout and text type because it helps them with their own use of persuasive techniques. There are similarities with analysing newspapers' use of language and design to appeal to the reader.

Taking it further

Get students to develop their own advertisements based on what they have learned through this exercise. For instance, students try and persuade another member of the class to follow a favourite sport, pick up a new hobby or to use a new app. If they decide to create an app there are opportunities here for linking with the computing curriculum.

Bonus idea ★

Alternatively you could use an incongruous font and discuss impact that way:

Thieves steal Christmas presents from children's hospital

Super fun for teens!

Ask students to bring in a selection of coloured print advertisements that are designed to appeal to a variety of audiences. Ask them to identify the following: the product, the image, visual features such as text size and colour, who the product appeals to and why. Try to ensure that they focus not simply on what is being advertised, but on how the product is being presented.

Students report back to the class. They should then select key words or phrases from the advertisements and discuss what response they are meant to provoke. Are personal pronouns used? What is being offered if someone were to buy this product? They will be familiar with the *purpose* of the form – to persuade – and many will have some idea of the intended *audience*, which will need just a little teasing out.

Encourage them to talk about *how* features are made to stand out, for example, through the use of bold or large type and the colours used. Ask them to analyse the difference between the messages which are conveyed through the following typefaces:

Thieves steal Christmas presents from children's hospital

Super fun for teens!

Connotation

"Reading between the lines. What's this really saying?"

Understanding connotation and implied meaning is a skill that makes reading more rewarding and makes students' writing more interesting. One way of approaching this topic is to think about the 'story' that is sitting behind the word or statement.

Display to the class a list of names of, for example, cars or soft drinks. The important thing is that the list contains product names that carry implied meaning and associations both negative and positive. Read through the list with students. Discuss some of the names, asking students for ideas about what the name suggests about the car or drink. Ask students to select three and briefly sketch a picture of each car or soft-drink container as they think best fits the name. For example, car names may include 'Rat', 'Tiger' 'Matador' or 'Cockroach' and soft drinks may include 'Sprint', 'VitFresh', 'Fizzbomb' or 'Swamp Juice'.

Next, ask students to feed back their ideas to the class and examine the connotations they picked up on from the product name. Note down any images or ideas that are most common or pertinent. Focus the class on the suggestions they have made and what connotations have been evoked by the product name. Ask students to identify which names from the list they felt were most and least successful as product names, identifying the connotations of each name and discussing the effects created.

Teaching tip

You can reverse the process of inferring the qualities implied by a name by asking students to look at an image either through a visualiser or IWB. For example, showing a picture of an apple you could ask students to suggest the qualities which could be drawn out and how this might translate into a name for the apple. From 'Golden Delicious' to 'Crunch Creator'.

Taking it further

Ask students to come up with examples of their own ideas of names for products that imply the qualities – the wilder the better!

Poetry

Part 9

Potty about poetry

"Painting is silent poetry and poetry is painting that speaks."
Plutarch

We need to encourage our students to enjoy the process and use their skills as readers, looking for clues and meaning.

Teaching tip

Use this simple introduction to structure and purpose as a springboard for a look into more complex forms – the sonnet, the villanelle, the ballad – giving students the tools with which to identify poetic form and comment upon the link between form and purpose.

Some students find that, while they may enjoy reading and writing poetry, writing *about* poetry can be a bit tricky. Students can be taught about some of the features of poetry such as rhyme, voice, rhythm, sound, structure and imagery through the following exercise. It is, though, important that we don't simply reduce poetry to a list of features but encourage students to engage with the impact of the text.

Short poems such as limericks can be a useful starting point for understanding rhyme and rhythm. Display a limerick on the IWB in prose form and read it to the class as prose, ignoring rhyme and rhythm. Ask students if they noted anything strange and then ask a volunteer to read it out. Most children will be able to identify the rhythm and rhyme of a limerick, so you should have many volunteers for this. Ask students to write out the limerick in their books in the correct format.

Taking it further

Using the rules they identified together as a guideline, students write their own limericks and read them to the class. Examples of limericks created by students can be found here: www.teachingideas.co.uk/english/limerick.htm. You could give some further support by giving line starters or ends.

Next, ask students to create a set of rules for limericks, for example, number of lines, rhyme scheme and rhythm, number of beats per line. They should also come up with some ideas about content and tone, for example, the first line introduces a person; the next three set up a situation; the final line acts as a punch line, and that the tone/purpose is humorous.

Rhythm and pace

"Knowing that the word 'rhythm' comes from the Greek for 'measured flow or movement' helped me to make the link with music."

It is very satisfying to make the links between music and poetry. The first poems we know about were sung with the lyre as accompaniment. Knowing this helps students understand the connection with the words 'lyric' and 'lyrical'.

Play students two pieces of music of different rhythms, for example, a slow song outlining love 'gone bad', and a fast-paced anthem of defiance or joy. As they listen to the music, ask students to write down any observations about the rhythm and to make note of any links they hear between the rhythm and the meaning of the music. Ask them to note if the rhythm changes at any point and why they think this happens; whether any words or phrases are repeated; and if this repetition has a corresponding rhythm change.

Give students a short list of themes or subjects and ask them to decide what kind of rhythm or pace would be most suitable for each, with reasons for their decisions. It is important here that links are made between structure and meaning. Next, distribute two short poems that have different and obvious patterns. Read out each poem in turn, emphasising rhythm. In pairs, ask students to work out how the rhythm is created, using their notes as guidance. Again, ask students to think about why a certain rhythm is used and how it influences or reinforces meaning. Select poems depending on the needs of the class: some will need straightforward poems where the links between form and meaning is clear, other students could be challenged by poetry that has more complex, irregular or changing patterns.

Teaching tip

To reinforce the idea of rhythm, ask students to tap along to a poem such as 'The Badger' by John Clare, which has a fast, insistent pace that mimics the chase described in the poem. 'Who's for the Game?' by Jessie Pope can also be used – its insistent, pacey rhythm reinforcing its figuring of war as play. Guide the students to comment on how the fast pace is created – word and line length, punctuation, sound and repetition. Observations should be noted on the board and on their own copies of the poem.

Taking it further

Encourage students to research the history of lyrics, tracing it back to the ancient Greeks. Ask them to explain the similarities and differences between music and poetry.

Let's imagine in rhyme!

"Imagery creates vivid pictures in the mind."

Imagery uses sensory details to create depth and richness in poetry. Skills developed elsewhere in English that help students understand connotation, atmosphere and metaphor are useful when looking at imagery in poetry.

Introduce the idea that imagery helps to create a picture for the reader. Provide students with two pictures and a number of strips of paper that have written on them descriptive images that relate to elements of the pictures. Try to provide students with a number of possible choices. For example, one strip could describe a 'pale, ghostly moon suspended in mist' whilst another could describe how 'the butter-yellow moon broke smiling through the sky'. In pairs, ask students to select and attach the descriptive images to the pictures in the place they think most fitting. Students share their ideas and give reasons for their choices. This activity could also be run using tablets if you have them, or an IWB. Develop this by giving students sets of different written images and asking them to draw the scene or character as they see it from the descriptive images given.

'The Fly' by Walter de la Mare is an excellent starting point for an examination of imagery in a whole poem. It is structured as a list of similes and can be used easily and effectively as a model. First, read through the poem with students and then give them one line to analyse in pairs. Ask them to consider what impression is being created by different similes, for example 'A rosebud like a featherbed'. Write or display each line on the board and ask students to give their ideas for that simile.

Sensational sounds

"Reading poetry aloud made all the difference to my students. Not only did the words and meaning come alive, but it also gave them greater confidence to read to one another."

Onomatopoeia and sound imagery provide students with a powerful way into discussing poetry. Poetry is often meant to be read aloud and sound can, therefore, play a big part in the impression created by a poem.

Display sets of onomatopoeic sounds and ask students to come up with what is being described, for example, 'buzz, rustle, buzz, shriek, buzz, thud, thud, slap, slap, shriek' – could describe a wasp chasing someone. Explain that the word 'onomatopoeia' comes from the Greek for 'making up a new word'.

Ask students to think about why certain sounds remind them of certain things, for example, school bells, car horns blaring, the sound of running water. Ask them to come up with a list of sounds from everyday life, for example, a busy supermarket, a football match or the beach. Ask them to share their ideas and use them to create sound poems to be read aloud, where they are encouraged to make them as alliterative and vivid as possible.

Students now need to focus on words which are not onomatopoeic, but which nonetheless create a particular sense impression. Remind students about alliteration and show them a selection of words that they have to pair up using alliteration as their guide. Next, ask students to write lines that use alliteration for a particular purpose, such as a lullaby or a pre-match team chant. Ask students to focus on the sounds they will use – soft, sibilant sounds for a lullaby and harder consonant sounds for the chant. Students share and discuss their work, exploring the effects created by sound.

Teaching tip

Use poems such as 'The Listeners' by Walter de la Mare, or 'Beach Music' by David Johnson to help students to make links between the sounds of the words and their meaning.

Taking it further

Ask students to choose one poem from www. thepoetrychannel.org. uk and to read it aloud to the class. Do they notice any differences? For example, what does Michael Rosen emphasise when he reads Philip Larkin's poem 'Born Yesterday'? What does the class notice when a student reads it aloud?

Poetry as story

"My students got the hang of a ballad when they realised that it is a simple story in verse."

Ballads have mass appeal and are easy to remember. This is because they are a vehicle for a story and have a lilting rhythm which links it back to its musical origins. You can use this musical link as a starter by giving students a song to listen to which has a strong narrative structure. Ask them to consider what is repeated, what the story is, why a story may be told in this form etc.

Taking it further

Ask students to focus on one or two of the questions then to provide longer more detailed responses. Each pair then feeds back their answer(s), which are then annotated on the displayed copy of the ballad and on students' own copies. This sort of task can be completed much more easily with tablets and an IWB.

Bonus idea ★

Ask students to have a go at writing their own ballad. It doesn't have to be perfect and should be treated as a chance to practise and play with ideas, words and rhythm. Before they do, ask them to look at some poems and identify which are ballads and why. From this, assemble a series of elements that make up a ballad, to help structure the students' own ballad writing.

Give the class copies of a ballad, such as 'La Belle Dame Sans Merci' by John Keats, written in prose form. You can choose a more modern ballad if you prefer, such as 'The Sad Story of Lefty and Ned'. Read aloud. Next, explain to students what a ballad is: simple story – originally passed on orally – that is event-driven rather than contemplative.

Put students into pairs or small groups and give each the ballad in verse form, but cut into separate stanzas. Ask the students to sequence the ballad before agreeing an order as a class. The ballad can be pasted to a piece of paper, large enough for students to annotate in their pairs. Read the poem again but this time as a class or asking students to read out a stanza each. Display a series of questions that deal with content and that ask students to look at structure, for example:

- What is the story of the poem? (No more than two sentences.)
- What do you think the mood or tone of the poem is? Why do you think that?
- Are any words or phrases repeated (refrain)? Why do you think it is repeated?
- Is the poem broken into stanzas? Are they the same length? Why?
- Do any of the lines rhyme?

Poetry on stage

"My class created an effective performance of 'A Case of Murder' as a mystery piece with armchair-seated narrator and sitting room set!"

This exercise increases engagement and understanding as the students move from reading to performance. Each time they put the meaning into a new context they gain new insights into the narrative poem.

You could use narrative poems such as the Key Stage 3 perennial 'The Highwayman' and 'A Case of Murder' by Vernon Scannell. 'The Highwayman' is a tale of passion and tragedy that has some very effective visual imagery. 'A Case of Murder' is similarly rich with imagery – both visual and aural – and has a slightly manic tone, which develops throughout the poem.

Read through the chosen poem with the class and focus on key images and features. Next, ask students to storyboard it. Drawing is not the focus here; what you are looking to create is a visual sense of the poem. Students will need to identify key narrative elements as well as imagery. Once this in completed, students work in groups to agree the best ways in which to visualise key elements of the poem.

Next, the groups could work on a performance of the poem. Group dynamics must be effective, so move students if necessary. Also, be sure that you are in an appropriate and safe space – it may be worth using the hall or a drama space for this activity.

Give the class some ideas about how to organise their performance. Do they want to use a single narrator, or a variety of voices for different elements? Will it be in the form of a news programme or a play? What atmosphere will they create? How? What images and sounds will they present? Each group then performs the poem.

Teaching tip

Record parts of the rehearsal and the final performances of the different groups. Show to the students and ask them to comment on how their understanding shifted as they rehearsed, collaborated refined to reach the final piece. This will help them to realise that deeper understanding comes from practice, redrafting and negotiating ideas with others.

Taking it further

This is a great opportunity to discuss with your students how to work effectively as a group. Get them to create a set of guidelines to follow for successful group work.

Drama

Part 10

Playing with plays

"Texts become meaningful when students take part in plays. Acting develops understanding and critical awareness."

Many students are not familiar with the conventions of drama and the explicit differences between a play and a novel, so they need opportunities to compare how these genres work in different ways.

Teaching tip

Create a class mind map on the key features of a play with examples from students' discussions as they note the differences between the structure of a play and a novel. Encourage them to make this as detailed as possible.

Students, including less skilled readers, generally enjoy reading plays as a class. This is because they are able to participate in reading, experience a variety of voices and have the chance to interpret texts from a character's perspective. You need to capitalise on this enjoyment if reading plays is to be as effective as possible.

Mind-map the students' ideas about the differences between a play and a novel. These should include textual aspects – how the text is presented on the page or the type of words used, for example, novels will have more descriptive detail and can shift quickly from place to place – as well as ideas about purpose and form, for example, in plays characters names are written on the left-hand side and no speech marks are used. Distribute extracts from a selection of novels and plays and ask students to identify which text type each extract is.

Get the class to agree on five key differences between plays and novels before listing each difference alongside an explanation as to why the difference exists and what purpose it serves, for example, students may conclude that novels are much more descriptive than plays, because for a play the audience can *see* characters and places and there is no need to describe them. Students share their thoughts.

Distribute a scene that has no stage directions whatsoever – from a play you are studying, a play that is new to the class or one devised by you. Explain what stage directions are (instructions for the actors on how to perform the story of the play). In pairs, ask students to add stage directions to the passage that will influence the way in which the scene is performed. Let students decide their own direction here or guide them though this. Stage directions should influence what actions are performed and how; how the stage and actors should look and how words are delivered.

Each pair swaps their annotated extract with another pair who then act out the scene following the new stage directions. Having observed all or a selection of performances, students write about two very different interpretations they have seen, noting how each was presented and how differences of mood and atmosphere were created. For example, a dark depressing piece could be conveyed through facial expressions, tone and pace of language. Encourage them to identify the clues.

Distribute to students the key events of a play in continuous prose. Ask students to break the play up into scenes. They must indicate why they have made a scene division – what indicators suggested it was necessary and what effect the division may have. This should lead to discussion about why most plays are divided into acts and scenes: ask students to write two sentences explaining their thoughts on the subject. If appropriate, students also offer their opinions as to why some plays are structured without scene divisions.

Taking it further

Ask students to devise a short play script of their own for a given series of events, characters, moods and so on. Make sure that they include stage directions. These needn't be very long. They can be given to another group to perform and then discuss.

Clues to expression

"I love reading plays out loud with masses of expression. We get the chance to exaggerate and to link the words with their meaning."

Students need to understand clues to expression found in texts. It is especially useful to use play texts to illustrate this because the expression in their voices will be heard.

Display several lines of speech that contain expression indicators such as question marks, exclamation marks and italics. Volunteers read each line, putting in the expression suggested by the expression indicator:

PAT: So I'm going to the party?

DAVID: You *do* have one for sale after all.

JOHN: She's gone to town!

Next, display the same lines, but with different indicators used and again, volunteers read the line with appropriate expression:

PAT: So *I'm* going to the party.

DAVID: You do have one for sale after all!

JOHN: She's gone to town?

Explain to the students that they are going to be using expression indicator techniques to transform a text from one literary form to another, in this case from play to prose. To reinforce ideas about the differences between plays and prose, ask students to transform a scene into prose. Be sure that students are aware of the differences: characters and setting have to be provided through description; speech marks have to be used when characters speak; body language is provided in prose and an omniscient narrator often describes how characters are feeling.

Taking it further

Students produce montages/posters which represent either the play as a whole, or particular scenes or acts. Each montage needs to include images that illustrate key themes, events or issues and a selection of words/phrases that are integral to the act/scene/play. Ask them to indicate where they have exaggerated or given additional expression to their section of the play. This could be through symbols or brief quotes. The design of the montage should be in keeping with the tone of the play. Allocate each group a different key scene to illustrate in a montage which can then be used as class display.

Stunning Shakespeare!

"I found that giving students examples of phrases which Shakespeare created and which are still used today was a great way to help them see how relevant his language is."

More often than not, students fear that the language of Shakespeare will prove too difficult. To tackle this, familiarise your class with Shakespearean language before they tackle a play.

Start by giving your students examples of commonly used phrases such as:

'It's all Greek to me' ('Julius Caesar')
'A pound of flesh' ('The Merchant of Venice')
'All's well that ends well' (from the play of the same name!)

Next, provide students with these pronouns: 'thee', 'thy', 'thou' and 'thine' and get them to translate simple sentences:

I will take you shopping. *I will take thee shopping.*
Your bedroom need to be tidied. *Thy bedroom needs to be tidied.*
You went skating. *Thou went skating.*

Note that 'thee' is used when 'you' is the object; 'thou' when 'you' is the subject. Students often enjoy this hybrid of Shakespearean and contemporary English and it is a great icebreaker.

Give students a piece of Shakespearean text to read, for example, an extract from the play they are going to study, or an unrelated piece of Shakespeare's work such as a sonnet. What is most important is that it is manageable, yet challenging. Read through the extract with the class and, in pairs, ask them to work out what it means. During class feedback, focus on any images or words that the class finds difficult.

Teaching tip

Ask students to choose their favourite short Shakespearean quote from a selection provided and get them to repeat it over several lessons. This could take the form of an extended register, so that when students answer their names, they also say their chosen quote.

Taking it further

Most students will be at least vaguely familiar with the stories of many of Shakespeare's plays. Ask them to mind-map their ideas on the board. Students then try to reduce their ideas to three key facts, for example, if the class is studying 'Romeo and Juliet', ask them to rewrite the prologue their own words.

Introducing Shakespeare

"I really enjoyed making the links between Shakespeare's plays and the kinds of dilemmas we still have today. Some of what he writes is really amusing as well!"

Shakespeare's stories may be 'timeless', but for many students this is obscured by the difficulty they experience in understanding seventeenth century English. When they are first getting to grips with Shakespeare, students often gain easier access to the text by re-figuring a play in a contemporary setting. This helps us draw narrative to the surface. It is by no means a simple substitution but rather a route into the play itself.

Taking it further

Ask the students to create Twitter accounts for the characters they are studying. They will need to create brief profiles and create comments with just 140 characters. They should try to keep 'in role' so that comments between Romeo and Juliet for example reflect what is happening in the play. Giving students different characters to tweet as can allow them to show how these characters would react differently to key events, for example. The Twitter accounts can be kept private to the class but provide a way for students to distil their ideas. It is important to keep a clear learning focus when using approaches such as these, otherwise the tweet becomes the thing rather than the play.

Re-set the main theme of the plays into a different context which can be more readily understood by students, for example, 'Macbeth' could be based on urban gangland power struggles; 'Romeo and Juliet' could be transposed to supporters of rival football teams. It doesn't have to be a modernisation of plot or context. It could be that you provide a route in by way of themes, dilemmas and feelings. You could focus in, for example, on an element that you think will capture their interest. This could be obedience to parents, loyalty to your friends, following your dream at the expense of others and so on.

Another way into the play is to emphasise the importance of opening scenes and what they can tell an audience about the play to come. For example, in 'Romeo and Juliet', take the opening scene and split the class in half, with one half taking the role of the Montagues and the other half the Capulets – to create tension ask the readers to leave their seats and face each other as they say their lines. If suitable, arrange the class along Capulet/Montague lines while they study the play.

What about the language?

"I had no idea that Shakespeare could be so cruel and funny!"

Helping students to see how colourful Shakespeare's language can be, provides a useful way into his language. The language of Shakespeare is not something that should be avoided! In doing so, we do him and our students a disservice. The language of his plays was, after all, intended to be accessible to everyone.

Shakespeare's plays are littered with insults. Some good examples can be found here: www.shakespeare-online.com/quotes/ shakespeareinsults. Present a sample of these insults together as a table and ask students to write in the empty column what they think the insults mean. For students who need additional support you could provide a list of insults along with translations for the students to pair up. Ask students to discuss the effect of the insults – what do they tell us? What kinds of words are used? How do they sound? This can act as an appetiser to some more engaged involvement with the language.

Another possibility is to select two short extracts showing contrasting language, for example, one that shows the language of love and one that shows the language of hate. Ask students to make detailed, guided comparisons, looking at types of image used, punctuation and sound. Students then select a line or image from each extract that they find most successful and write three lines explaining why they found it so effective. Make these into illustrated 'image maps' of the play, whereby key images from each scene are illustrated alongside the appropriate quotation. Students can be asked to transform these extracts into a different type of text, a letter perhaps or an interview. These transformative tasks, if focused sufficiently, can help them demonstrate and deepen their understanding.

Teaching tip

Getting students to engage with the text quite early is important. The greater the distance, the more students feel that it is something to be scared of. The introduction can be through themes, language or characters. It just needs to be an early engagement.

Taking it further

Allocate a character to groups of students who will focus on that character either for the duration of the play or for specific scenes and tasks. For example, in 'Romeo and Juliet' the characters of Tybalt, Benvolio, Mercutio and Romeo could be allocated to specific groups who track their characters during the pivotal fight scene in Act 3. Each group then feeds back to the class, using quotations to back up their observations of their character's actions, intentions and thoughts. Encourage them to include as many insults as possible.

Shakespeare on screen

"Watching different versions of 'Romeo and Juliet' was helpful. Our teacher asked us to think about the similarities and differences which made us think about how the play had been interpreted."

Film and music can be valuable assets in the classroom, but need to be used effectively. Simply sitting the class in front of the television for two lessons is not going to have much impact on their learning. Use selected extracts, and make it clear that what is shown is an interpretation rather than a definitive version. I would also advise against showing students the film version of the play before they have read it. After all, *spoiler alert!* once you know that they both die in the end, reading 'Romeo and Juliet' loses some of its pull!

When using a film version of a play, think about how to use it to best focus students on key elements of the play. You could, say, show several versions of a key scene – the fight scene in act 3 of 'Romeo and Juliet', for example – and ask students to decide which best fits their own interpretations. Students could comment on how characters are represented and any differences between the play and the film. If possible, use a variety of different versions to enable students to compare and also to avoid them associating the play so closely with one film version.

Play appropriate background music quietly when key scenes are being read or just before. This helps to set the atmosphere and make the scene more memorable for many students. Then get students to choose their own soundtrack for selected scenes using music provided by you. Give students a list of scenes and ask them to write which piece of music is most fitting for a given scene, along with the reasons behind their selection.

Taking it further

Ask students to script and perform a courtroom scene of the play they have been studying. They should think about costume, music, setting and direction.

On with the play

"Believe it or not, I really enjoyed going through the play looking for key ideas and features. It made it more interesting to spot what was going on!"

Students should be made aware of key themes, storyline, characters and images throughout the play. Understanding features such as the aside and the soliloquy, and conventions such as tragedy and comedy are essential. Close reading of key scenes will help unpack the elements of the play. How you organise this can have a real impact upon students' understanding.

You may want to consider at first whether you intend to read the play in its entirety or only key scenes selected thematically or with a focus on a character, for example. This will be informed by the overall aim of the study. Once you have decided that, think about how you will organise the actual reading of the play. You may choose to use a number of different approaches depending on focus, need and so on. For example, for some early, difficult or important passages, a teacher may be best placed to focus students on meaning and provide a model. For certain key scenes, you may feel that students need to engage with the language of the characters.

Consider the following possibilities and think of places where they might be the most useful approach and also of any limitations:

- Students allocated roles to read throughout duration.
- Teacher reads key parts.
- Students act out key scenes in character.
- Teacher reads out stage directions.
- Teacher reads using different voices for different characters.
- Students switch roles.
- Teacher reads whilst students act.

Bonus idea ★

Students collect information throughout the reading of the play and use it to construct a sensational news story. Their story should have a specific angle, comments from characters and feature a number of incidents prominently. This should be prepared with a particular news outlet in mind – the approach will differ according to whether it is being written for the BBC News app, the *Daily Mail* newspaper or for the class blog. Again, it helps if the students are writing for an authentic audience.

Dramatic English!

"Getting active gets us to think!"

Techniques from drama are great ways of taking the learning deeper. In these exercises students have to think about and justify their answers, giving them richer language both for speaking and writing.

Hot seating is a great way to explore character and can also contribute to a speaking and listening assessment. Both the student in the hot seat and the rest of the class need to have considerable knowledge of the character for this to be effective. A student assumes the role of a named character in a studied text and answers questions from the class. If the questions tend to be centred on information found in the text, extend the task to include broader questions and answers which are 'in character'. For this type of task to have real value, students must understand that they are 'in character', and what this means so be sure to explain this at the outset.

Tableau is an activity helps students grasp a sense of situation and atmosphere, as well as an understanding of the role of body language in creating a particular impression. A tableau functions like a staged snapshot; students create a 'freeze frame' of a situation and hold it. The most effective of these create a real sense of the scene and reactions to it. Students produce tableaux of different key scenes for others to identify, or each group produces a tableau of the same scene and notes the differences.

Taking it further

Drama techniques used in the English classroom, are not confined to text-related activities but can be used to explore character, situation, style and so on as part of a focus on language.

Role play

"We used role play as a way to enter into the perspective of another character and it was so interesting to see things from the inside."

Role play is a great device to explore elements of the curriculum connected to both language and literature. Students adopt a role and interact with one another, exploring the limits and qualities of their given role and its attendant viewpoint.

Make sure students understand that role play is not about acting skills but draws on their life experiences. For example, a courtroom scene is just as effective to explore issues of blame in 'Romeo and Juliet' as it is to provide a convincing framework for a debate on school-leaving age.

As a language-based exercise, put students into small groups and give them a card with a situation and list of suggested characters. Students then write their own short plays based on the information given. Be sure to direct their focus on how the play will begin and end, how each character will feel, how this is to be represented in both words and actions and any drama techniques they may wish to include. If possible, ask each group to consider ideas for set and costume and to have reasons for their choices. Assess this as a voice performance or, if time and space allow, as a play.

Taking it further

Extend the range of characters who are involved and who might have a point of view in a scene you are considering. What might they see, what might they be thinking? What other additional insights can we gain from working in this way?

Bonus idea

Students create their own news programme based on a literary text or as a language exercise. Ensure that the different elements of the programme are included, such as studio presenters, local news, outside reports and a weather report, and that differences in tone, language and so on are noted.

Spelling, Grammar and Punctuation

Part 11

The secret to spelling

"My students often lacked confidence in spelling certain words and I wanted to help them to get to grips with some troublesome words. These come up frequently, so I told them it was worth spending time getting these right."

While some spelling errors are quite unfathomable, there are certain words which come up time and again. It's worth helping your students to get to grips with these if they want to write like a 'pro'!

Here is a list of ten of the most commonly misspelled words:

amount, beginning, definitely, friend, immediately, independent, library, occasion, sincerely, separate.

Use this list or, with the help of your students, create a list that meets the needs of your class. You can use this stage as a spelling test or vocabulary exercise. Ask students to use this list to start a spelling diary at the back of their books to record spelling corrections and troublesome words.

Common spelling patterns or rules can also cause spelling to go awry. Give students the following rules to copy, and test them on each section. The following tasks and exercises help to clarify some of the most frequently misunderstood spelling rules.

The disappearing 'e'

Why does 'confuse' become 'confusing' and 'care' become 'caring', yet care keeps the 'e' when it becomes 'careful'? Generally, if a *suffix* (letters added to the end of a word to change its meaning) starts with a *vowel*, the 'e' will be removed before the suffix is added. For example:

believe + able = believable

investigate + ion = investigation

move + ing = moving.

However, when a suffix starting with a *consonant* is added to a word which ends with an 'e', the 'e' will be kept and the suffix added on. For example:

engage + ment = engagement

hope + less = hopeless

secure + ly = securely.

Swimming and jumping?

Why do some words have a double letter added in the middle? Usually, if a word has *one syllable* and ends with *one consonant*, the last consonant will be *doubled*. For example:

skip = one syllable and one consonant at end = skipping

hit = one syllable and one consonant at end = hitting

jump = one syllable and two consonants at end = jumping

climb = one syllable and two consonants at end = climbing.

Sentence types

"Going from simple to complex can make things more interesting."

Students' writing is livelier and has more energy if they can build on simple one-clause sentences to use a variety of sentence types. This will also sharpen their understanding of texts.

Simple sentences

If necessary, remind students that a sentence usually contains a subject and a verb. A 'simple sentence' is usually a clause that has one main verb and subject. The verb says what the subject is doing.

Compound sentences

Ask students for examples of connectives and conjunctions to help them extend sentences. The most commonly used are 'and', 'but' and 'or' but they could also use: 'however', 'furthermore', 'in addition to' etc. Display pairs of simple sentences which are jumbled up, such as:

It was cold outside. The dog was covered in mud.

Richard was great at football. We stayed indoors.

The sofa was filthy. He was terrible at rugby.

Ask students to work out which sentences go together. Then ask them to use a connective to join the pairs together to make one long sentence. Explain that these are called 'compound sentences' and are made of two parts of a sentence called a clause, joined by a connective. Each clause could be a sentence on its own but linking them together makes them more interesting.

Complex sentences

A complex sentence has more than one idea. So it's like a compound sentence, but the ideas are not equal. This is because one part is like a simple sentence and it makes sense on its own. The other part needs something else for it to make sense. If we look at the sentence below we see that the first part makes sense on its own, but if we take it away then the second part doesn't make sense:

<u>The school shut early</u> after the storms.

This is why we call this second part of a sentence a 'dependent clause', because it depends on the first bit to make sense. Words like 'because', 'since', 'after', 'when' link the two together.

It is important that we give students the skills to use these sorts of sentences to improve their own writing, rather than simply be able to identify them. They need to be given opportunities to explore and use different sentence types.

Write a number of different sentence types on pieces of card or use the IWB to generate them. Students then need to pick five cards. The five sentence types, in the order in which they were selected, should be used as a template for a piece of writing. It may be: a complex sentence, a complex sentence, a simple sentence, a compound sentence, a simple sentence. You can, of course, mix this up as their skills develop to include, for example, direct speech.

Taking it further

The word 'noun' comes from the ancient Greek, *onoma* and Latin *nomen* both meaning 'name'. Ask students to research the words 'subordinate'; 'clause'; 'dependent'; 'adjective'; 'adverb'. They could then produce a display which shows the 'roots' of these words. Students can provide their own examples for each. Their learning will go deeper if they are expected to refer to these regularly.

Adding adjectives

"Adding power to words."

Recognition and use of adjectives in writing will enhance students' reading and understanding skills as well as their own writing.

Explain to students that adjectives are words that give us more information about a noun, for example:

The cat sat on the mat.
The <u>fat</u> cat sat on the <u>dirty</u> mat.

Now ask students to add adjectives to the following sentences.

The boy bought some trousers.
The house was empty.

To develop this exercise, give students passages from a class text and ask them to delete the adjectives. Ask them to talk about the difference when the adjectives have been taken out. Alternatively, get students to describe something using adjectives only. For example, 'I am green, rectangular, chipped and scratched' to describe a classroom door.

It is important that students know how adjectives are used in non-fiction texts, too. One way of doing this is to use advertisements, holiday brochures or property descriptions from estate agents. Again, remove the adjectives from the texts and ask students to say whether there is any difference in impact. Then ask students to put in their own adjectives. Remind the class to focus on how adjectives can be used as a form of persuasion.

Which noun?

"Getting names right!"

Most students will have been taught about the parts of speech during Key Stage 2. However, it is a good idea to check their understanding, both to reinforce their learning and to establish the needs of your class. The following can be used as an aide-memoiré or as the foundation for class exercises.

'Nouns' are naming words. They are used to name things, people or ideas/feelings and are often the most important part of a sentence. Look at the following sentences. Without nouns, it is difficult to make sense of them.

The_____went to the____to get some____.

_____is a good for a____.

Students fill in the gaps and then compare the different sentences they come up with.

There are three types of noun:

1 **Concrete nouns**: these name objects you can see or touch; such as 'book', 'glove', 'boy', 'car'.
2 **Proper nouns**: these name particular people, places or things; such as 'Paul', 'Leeds', 'America', 'Harry Potter'.
3 **Abstract nouns**: these name feelings or ideas; such as 'anger', 'happiness', 'rest', 'tomorrow'.

Ask students to look again at the nouns they chose to fill in the gaps. What type of noun have they used?

Tell students that a good way to remember the difference between concrete and abstract nouns is that concrete nouns are experienced through the senses while abstract nouns are not.

Taking it further

These activities can be extended and developed as you see fit. For example, read short passages and identify noun types or replace them with others of the same type. Or tie this work in with other aspects of writing, such as creating narrative, by emphasising how different noun choices can create very different effects.

Pronoun practice

"Understanding the idea that a pronoun stands in for something else helps my students make their writing more efficient."

An understanding of pronouns will help students' writing to become more interesting and also improve their analysis of different texts.

Teaching tip

Create a mnemonic to help another class remember what pronoun means. For example: 'p' is for 'in **p**lace of'; 'r' is for '**r**ather than'; 'o' is for 'instead **o**f'; 'n' is for alternative **n**ame'; 'o' is for '**o**ther replacement word'; 'u' is for '**u**sed instead of'; 'n' is for 'avoid repeating the **n**oun'.

Remind students that pronouns are used in place of nouns and will help make their writing more interesting and varied. Display a short piece of writing such as the following in which no pronouns are used:

Paul went to town to buy some shoes. Paul saw Carol and Paul and Carol went shopping together. Carol wanted to buy Paul a birthday present but Carol didn't know what Paul wanted. Paul and Carol stopped for a coffee and Paul and Carol's friend Ian saw Paul and Carol. Ian wanted some cake and so Paul bought Ian and Carol a slice each.

Ask for a volunteer to read the piece aloud, substituting every instance of 'Paul' or 'Carol' with a pronoun from the following displayed list: 'me', 'my', 'I', 'mine', 'she', 'her', 'hers', 'he', 'his', 'our', 'we', 'us', 'they', 'them', 'you', 'your', 'it'. Students should note that if they only use pronouns the passage becomes as difficult to understand as with only nouns. The identity of the subject becomes lost and meaning becomes obscured. In pairs, ask students to rewrite the passage again, using a mixture of pronouns and proper nouns so that the meaning is clear throughout, but excessive repetition is avoided.

Taking it further

Ask students sort pronouns into different groups, for example, singular/plural, to describe people and objects.

Adverb charades!

"Adding colour to action through adverbs is incredibly helpful. My students can immediately see the difference it makes to the quality of their work."

Adverbs make writing more effective. While they can give information about a verb – when (for example, 'yesterday') and where (for example, 'over there') something occurs, students will be more familiar initially with adverbs used to describe how (for example, 'happily') a verb is undertaken.

Prepare strips of paper in two colours, for example, write individual verbs separately on blue strips of paper and adverbs on green strips. Place each set in separate containers and call willing students out in turn to pick out one verb and one adverb from the containers. Students then act out the combined phrase without mentioning either word, and the rest of the class guess what verb is being acted out. Combinations may be relatively straightforward, for example, 'skip happily' or unusual, for example, 'fish loudly'.

To consolidate the notion of 'how' and to introduce the 'where' and 'when' aspects of adverb use, give a number of verb phrases – as a written or verbal task – and ask them to add an adverb that addresses how, when and where that task is done:

I play football enthusiastically. (How)

I play football outside. (Where)

I play football tomorrow. (When)

Teaching tip

To check that students understand the terms learned thus far, ask them to work in groups of four. The first person asks the second to choose a noun, the third to choose a verb and the fourth to choose an adverb. The first person has to act out the meaning of the whole sentence.

Choose a connective

"Let's join things up!"

Understanding a variety of connectives or conjunctions can help students move away from stilted, single-clause sentences and make their writing more interesting and sophisticated.

Connectives will help students to move away from over-reliance on 'and', which can only be a bonus for both student and teacher! Students are not always familiar with the range of connectives nor with the relationship between the two joined elements, which is suggested by choice of connective. To demonstrate this, display sentences such as the following:

Pat went to town and it was raining.

Pat went to town because it was raining.

Pat went to town although it was raining.

Ask students to work out how the different connectives have altered the meaning of the sentence and which makes most sense to them. Give students three sentences to complete using the connective which they feel fits best, for example:

I have to stay in my aunt is visiting.

Our food was horrible we had a nice time anyway.

Andrew was happy Jim came along and ruined it.

Students then write two sentences with a missing connective and pass them to the person next to them to complete. To reinforce this, students then write five sentences describing their day, using a different connective in each one.

Playing with verbs

"Those powerful action words."

Students will be familiar with verbs from Key Stage 2 but some revision may be necessary along with some further work looking at verb choice and vocabulary. Remind students that verbs are 'doing' words: they tell us about what someone or something is doing. Some verbs are plain to see, such as 'jumping' or 'laughing', while others are not, such as 'thinking' or 'remembering'.

Ask students to write down how many things they 'did' yesterday. Many will be common to the class, such as talking or eating. Display a selection of these and pick one as a category heading. As a whole-class task, ask students to come up with as many alternative or related words as they can under this heading:

Eating: chewing, stuffing, swallowing, gnawing, gobbling, nibbling

Ask students, do the different words have different connotations?

Once this has been completed, select three more verb headings for which students can create 'word banks' and ask them to choose one of their own. Students feed back to the class and create a class word bank. Students then select verbs from the word bank to complete sentences such as:

Lucy_____to school.

Each sentence has to be written twice, each time using verbs with different connotations. The task aims to encourage students to think about verb choice both in their own writing and in that of others. By using different verbs they are able to see how the meaning and emphasis of a sentence changes. Rather than simply identifying what a verb is, this task focuses instead on what it does.

Teaching tip

Encourage students to use a thesaurus to find alternative verbs to add to the class word bank.

Taking it further

Extend this task by selecting situations, characters or effects and asking students to select an appropriate verb. With some students, you may then focus on the inappropriate or unexpected verb, and ask them to discuss the effect this may create.

The crafty comma

"The versatile punctuation mark."

The comma is often misunderstood and is frequently seen scattered randomly over the page or not seen at all. Students need to grasp how the comma affects meaning. Using commas accurately and consistently will help students make their written work more powerful.

Display two sentences such as the following, using a different colour for commas (any sentence can be used here as long the comma changes the meaning):

The boys who were cold and tired were sent back. (Only the cold and tired boys were sent back.)

The boys, <u>who were cold and tired</u>, were sent back. (All of the boys were cold and tired and were sent back.)

Underline 'who were cold and tired' and explain to students that this part of the sentence is extra information, and so commas are used to separate it from the main part of the sentence. The sentence should make complete sense without the extra information.

Students need then to look at how commas can be used to separate items on a list. Show them a sentence where the commas are missing and ask a volunteer to add commas to the list, for example:

She went to buy pasta bread oranges cat food sugar and cheese.

Ask students to write their own lists which are to be punctuated by their partner. To extend this task, include compound sentences that consist of two clauses separated by a comma. Give the class sentences or whole passages to punctuate.

Apostrophes

"Showing something is missing."

The apostrophe can cause all sorts of problems. Some students see them as a decorative flourish that adorns words ending in 's', while some will steer well clear of them altogether.

The rules for using apostrophes are fairly straightforward but they need to be taught explicitly if they are going to really stick. There are two main ways to use apostrophes. The first is explained here and the second in idea 97.

Apostrophes can indicate missing letters. This is seen when two words are joined together to make one. For example:

I am *becomes* I'm.

He is *becomes* he's.

Did not *becomes* didn't.

The missing letter is replaced with an apostrophe, to indicate where the letter was taken from. This makes meaning clearer and helps us to avoid confusing words such as 'were' and 'we're'. Ask your class to rewrite the following sentences using words with apostrophes:

Julie <u>is not</u> going to the beach.

<u>I cannot</u> see the stage.

The floor <u>was not</u> very clean.

Now do the reverse. Ask students to write out the following sentences in full, replacing the apostrophe with the missing letters:

<u>He's</u> a good footballer.

Natalie <u>hadn't</u> been to Greece before.

<u>It's</u> a long time until my next holiday.

More on apostrophes

"We learned that an apostrophe is a way to show that something belongs."

The second way to use apostrophes usually causes the most confusion, and students need to be taught explicitly where to place the apostrophe rather than just the rule.

The second use of the apostrophe is to indicate when something belongs to someone or something. This is seen when an apostrophe is put in immediately after the owner and an 's' is added too, for example, 'Kate's bag'. If the owner already ends in 's', most of the time you will add 's, for example, 'Chris's ball'. However, there is an exception to this - if the owner already ends in an 's', and when it is spoken aloud you don't sound out the added 's', then you do not have to add the 's'; for example, the boys' room (*not* the boys's room). But this is the cause of some debate and it depends on your own style. So, the general rule is: if it sounds right without the pronounced 's' then don't include it, but if the extra 's' is audible, it is generally included. As long as you are consistent, you will not confuse your students!

A simple way to remember when to put in an apostrophe is to ask the question: To whom or what does it belong? Ask students to put the apostrophe in immediately after the answer, for example:

Item	To whom does it belong?	Apostrophe inserted
The chefs hat	The chef	The chef's hat
Chris hair	Chris	Chris's hair
The boys changing room	The boys	The boys' changing room
The girls bag	The girl	The girl's bag

Once this has been done, ask the class questions to check understanding and ask them to rewrite sentences with an apostrophe by going through the process of asking the question: 'To whom or what does it belong to?':

The howl of the dog was pitiful.

The face of the mountain was treacherous.

Students then write five apostrophe-free sentences of their own and pass them to their partner to punctuate.

There are, of course, some very tricky examples. Where would the apostrophe go on a sentence describing the guitar belonging to the best guitarist in year 10? Would we use it or, sometimes, does it seem more clear to write without using the apostrophe? It may be worth exploring this with your students, once, of course, they have a secure understanding of the basics.

Finally, you can have some fun seeing how the apostrophe can change the meaning of a sentence:

My brother's friend's bikes. (I have one brother who has one friend)

My brothers' friends' bikes. (I have many brothers who have many friends)

My brothers' friend's bikes. (I have many brothers and they have one friend)

My brother's friends' bikes. (I have one brother and he has many friends).

Taking it further

Ask students to research the different uses of apostrophes and to evaluate some of the resources available to teach apostrophes by looking at some of the following sites: www.bbc. co.uk/skillswise/topic/ punctuation/resources/l1 and www.skillsworkshop. org/resources/ apostrophes-1.
Are these helpful? What could they do to make them better? Ask them to create their own resource to help other classes.

"Speech marks"

"When we worked together through how to get speech marks in the right place, students could see how straightforward it is. Now they remind themselves by saying 'I'm talking to you!'"

The use of direct speech in a piece of text, when done well, has many merits: characters can develop their own voices; students can show understanding of more complex, internal punctuation and writing is injected with more energy and variety.

Teaching tip

It is always worth getting students to practise what they have just learnt as they will enjoy applying new skills in different contexts. Ask students to find some dialogue in a book they are reading. Working in pairs they need to find three or four sentences, remove the speech marks and give the sentences to their partner to read aloud. Ask them to compare how speech marks make a difference to the sense.

Unfortunately, writing direct speech accurately can cause students significant problems: speech marks may be used, but in the wrong place; capitalisation is often forgotten and internal punctuation can be a mystery. It seems that because there are a few rules attached to the writing of speech, many students become confused and apply them inconsistently.

One of the most common and easily-remedied problems lies in deciding where to put speech marks. Students often place them indiscriminately around every word connected to speech. For example,

"Simon said I am not going to school and you can't make me."

A quick and effective way to rectify this is to write a number of unpunctuated sentences containing direct speech. Read out the parts of the sentence that are not direct speech yourself, and get volunteers to read out what is actually said. Underline this both on the board and in students' books. For example:

Simon said <u>why should I go to school</u>

<u>Well then</u> replied Jo <u>please yourself</u>

Students then put speech marks in place, using the underlining as a guide.

Punctuation and direct speech

"I wanted to find a way of reminding students to use punctuation correctly, so that their work was clearer and above all accurate. I told them this was all about producing professional prose!"

Students often need to be reminded about simple punctuation rules that are taught throughout school, for example, that a sentence starts with a capital letter and that speech should start with one too.

Ask students to start any speech in their writing with a capital letter, no matter where it occurs in a sentence (you could use this as a continuation of the exercise from idea 98):

Simon said "Why should I go to school"

"Well then" replied Jo "please yourself"

To keep punctuation rules simple, ensure that students remember to place a punctuation mark – question mark, full stop, comma or exclamation mark – at the end of speech *inside* the speech marks. Use a number of simple examples such as those below and allow students to select which punctuation mark they think fits best.

"What's for tea" asked Julie.

Matthew shouted "I won't play then"

"Why don't you come to the cinema"

Teaching tip

Take two extracts from a text and divide the class into two groups. Each group should work in pairs removing all punctuation. Ask students to swap the edited texts and get them to put in the missing punctuation. This will encourage them to look closely at the meaning and purpose of capital letters, commas, exclamation marks , apostrophes and speech marks.

Taking it further

Ask students to look at an earlier piece of work and improve the punctuation for clarity and meaning.

Refining direct speech

"My students were forgetting that their work has to make sense for the reader: they were running their sentences together and they needed to learn ways to show what was happening."

Students must learn how and when to use punctuation (usually a comma) as well as speech marks to separate the direct speech from the speech tag. This is to help the reader understand what has been written.

Remind students that a comma is always needed when the speech tag comes at the start of the sentence, but a comma is not needed if direct speech ends with an exclamation mark, full stop or question mark.

Simon said, "Why should I go to school?"

"Well then," replied Jo, "please yourself."

"Where is the canteen?" asked Ishmael.

Provide a number of example sentences for students to punctuate. For example:

Approaching the house the old man wondered where did I put my keys

What happened there said the boy to his mother

The final rule to refine direct speech is to start a new line for a new speaker, remembering to put the whole sentence on a new line, not simply the spoken words.

Once these rules have been established, encourage students to develop their writing by, for example, selecting interesting verbs for speech rather than relying on 'said'.

Also available now:

The bestselling title *100 ideas for Secondary Teachers: Outstanding Lessons* by Ross Morrison McGill.

Written by the most followed teacher on twitter in the UK, @TeacherToolkit, this book is a must have for every secondary teacher looking for new ideas to embed into their lessons to make them outstanding every day.

'I used the 5 minute lesson plan . . . to prepare for my interview in my training year. It really helped my to focus on what I wanted to achieve and ensure that I showed the school the best of what I had to offer. I got the job and I can't wait to use the 5 minute lesson plan in my training year. Thanks @TeacherToolkit!'

Danielle Manning, History NQT

Join the conversation on Twitter by searching for #100ideas.